No Worries

Spiritual and Mental Health Counseling for Anxiety

ELAINE LEONG ENG, MD

What People Are Saying

As a book division consultant, I reviewed and approved the publication of the first edition of this book in 2000. Little did I know that it would find its way to a church in Paris, a small hospital library in Niger, a coffee table in Japan, or to Taiwan in a Chinese version. In all these settings, it proved to be a source of mental health education for many sufferers of anxiety and for those who care for and love them. Moreover, it has served as a training text for countless students in pastoral and mental health counseling and audiences concerned about psychological health.

I believe that this updated version of Dr. Eng's classic book will be a source of comfort, hope, and knowledge to many, including those who struggle with anxiety and those who wish to help. I applaud her creation of another life-changing book that will be a long-sought-for oasis of relief and peace.

~ **Harold G. Koenig, MD**
Professor of Psychiatry & Behavioral Sciences
Duke University Medical Center
Durham, North Carolina

It is so helpful to have a guide book for lay people in the church who want to come alongside people with mental illness but don't know how to do it without getting completely overwhelmed. Dr. Eng gives the optimal model of "wrap-around care." She includes the medical professional, the professional counselor, and the church family in ministering to the one who finds life harder than most.

Dr. Eng also nicely de-mythologizes the inner life of the mentally ill by showing that all of us worry, are depressed, stressed, and anxious at some point in our lives. Not staying stuck in that way of thinking is the key to mental health. Pointing out that the one with on-going anxiety and depression is not hopeless and needs the Body of Christ to be there for them, allows the lay person in the church to be a listener and encourager without feeling guilty about setting boundaries.

~ **Dr. Robert Long**
missionary pediatrician (retired)
and **Judy Long, MA** *(Counseling)*
currently doing member care together in Asia

This book is a "must read" for Christian leaders who wish to understand how the mind works and, when impaired, can be properly diagnosed, treated, and brought back into wholeness. I travel all over the world. I see fellow believers suffering from different forms of anxiety and worry. Dr. Eng's book gives me tools to recognize when people are suffering and how to encourage them to get the help they need.

~ Jeff Seigel
President of Global Youth Baseball Federation, Inc.,
and New York Regional Director for Chosen People Ministries

This book is a godsend for providing practical advice about how to include biblical principles in treating anxiety disorders. Dr. Elaine Eng does a superlative job using case studies to illustrate various anxiety disorders and how they should be managed. This is a terrific resource for learning to manage anxiety among Christian workers, and how to do so in a sensitive and God-centered manner. Dr. Eng presents an outstanding discussion about how biblical principles integrate with cognitive behavioral therapy, and the power of Scripture to overcome the negative thoughts that can fuel patterns of anxiety.

~ **Meredith Hawkins, MD, MS**
Professor of Medicine
(Harold and Muriel Block Chair in Medicine)
Director, Global Diabetes Institute
(Co-Director, Einstein Diabetes Research Center)
Albert Einstein College of Medicine
Bronx, New York

No Worries: Spiritual and Mental Health Counseling for Anxiety is an excellent tool for pastors, missionaries, and seminarians. My dear colleague, Dr. Elaine Eng, has done a masterful job of integrating psychology with good biblical truth. The case studies and overall content will be extremely helpful to both those in ministry and those in need of ministry. I joyfully recommend this book to the professors and students in my seminary and to pastors and leaders everywhere.

~ **Dr. Ron Walborn**
Dean; Alliance Theological Seminary
Nyack, New York

No Worries

**Spiritual and
Mental Health
Counseling
for Anxiety**

ELAINE LEONG ENG, MD

NO WORRIES
Spiritual and Mental Health Counseling for Anxiety
by Elaine Leong Eng, MD
Copyright© 1996, Revision 2014 Elaine Leong Eng, MD
(Original Title: Martha, Martha) Library of Congress

Published by:
Healthy Life Press • 2603 Drake Drive • Orlando, FL 32810
www.healthylifepress.com

Designer: Judy Johnson

Printed in the United States of America

Library of Congress Cataloging-in-Publication Data
Eng, Elaine Leong, MD
No Worries: Spiritual and Mental Health Counseling for Anxiety

ISBN 978-1-939267-86-3
1. Anxiety; 2. Anxiety – Spiritual Counseling; 3. Anxiety – Mental Health Counseling

All Scripture quotations, unless otherwise indicated, are taken from The Holy Bible, New International Version® NIV®. Copyright © 1973, 1978, 1984, 2011 by Biblica, Inc.® Used by permission. All rights reserved worldwide. Scripture references marked NASB are taken from the New American Standard Bible. Copyright© 1960, 1962, 1963, 1968, 1971, 1972, 1973, 1975, 1977 by the Lockman Foundation. Used by permission. Scripture references marked KJV are from the King James Version.

Capitalization of pronouns related to deity follows *The Christian Writer's Manual of Style* (Grand Rapids: Zondervan, 2004). In biblical quotes, capitalization of pronoun related to deity follows the translation used in that passage.

This book is not intended to be used for diagnosis or treatment of any medical condition, or as medical advice. Readers should obtain medical advice, including diagnosis and treatment, from their personal physicians. Any use of the information provided in this book is at the user's risk. Neither the author nor the publisher shall be liable for any untoward results from the use of this information.

The opinions expressed in this book are those of the author, and may or may not represent the official views of Healthy Life Press.

The examples in this book are based on true cases, but they are composites. Every effort has been made to protect patient confidentiality; therefore, any similarity in case examples to any person, living or dead, is unintentional.

Photo of the author on the back cover is courtesy ofAndres Valenzuela Photography: *www.andresvalenzuela.com.*

Dedication

THIS BOOK IS DEDICATED TO THE LATE DR. CRAIG ELLISON, PHD,
founder of the Alliance Graduate School of Counseling
and beloved professor, psychologist, and
mentor to countless individuals.

Acknowledgements

SPECIAL THANKS ARE OWED TO NYACK COLLEGE FOR THEIR KIND SUPPORT and research grant. I am grateful to my colleagues and students for their encouraging, prayerful, and pragmatic contributions in the preparation of the manuscript. The following people deserve special applause for their tirelessness and willingness to assist in helping with this project: Elizabeth Dahlberg-Lee, Carmen Lau, Jeannine Brown, Dr. Deanna Kwan, Dr. Carol Robles, and Dr. Marcia Lucas.

Table of Contents

Publisher's Preface

QUITE RIGHTLY, THE TIME WE LIVE IN HAS BEEN CALLED BY MANY "THE Age of Anxiety." This pervasive angst is the background noise of life, both within the church and outside it. If an angel choir were to light up the sky around Bethlehem these days, some would hear the words, "Fear not . . ." or in modern lingo "No worries . . . for unto you was born a savior. . . ." But others would wonder if a bomb or missile had exploded. Either way, the whole world would know about it in a nanosecond, live and in color.

Against this backdrop comes a psychiatrist packing a dose of reality mixed with medicine and faith: "Anxiety may be rampant," she might admit calmly, "but the Prince of Peace is still in charge. We can trust Him with our cares, and we can also invite others to do the same. And in that process, is it not most prudent to use all the weapons in our arsenal of hope, including counseling and proven medical treatments, to help those who are discouraged, depressed, wounded, or hurting to find healing?"

Have we not all known sincere brothers and sisters, pastors and choir directors who were excessively anxious, or depressed, obsessed with one thing or another, or afraid of one thing or another? Not only so, but mental illness of this ilk is sometimes incorrectly spiritualized. For example, I once knew an older woman, quite revered by other older female members of her church, who cleaned the cracks between the floorboards in her home on a regular basis with a toothbrush.

And I well recall how during my time as a pastor, one couple seemed to experience more than the standard ups and downs of life. Their peaks and valleys were quite unpredictable, and I never could quite find a key to helping them in any significant way. When we met together for "counseling," it was sometimes like tag-team mud wrestling. Afterward, I would slough my way home to the parsonage trying to figure out why I was covered in mud.

Later, I learned about their particular disorder and the challenge it can present when just one spouse is afflicted. When both struggle, yet both claim to be believers and that they really do want help, now that's a pastor's nightmare, at least it was so way back then when today's treatments were just wishful thinking in the minds of those who longed to help believers suffering with one form or another of mental illness.

So how refreshing it is to have the privilege of publishing a book whose goal is to help pastors, counselors, and other people-helpers identify symptoms of common disorders related to anxiety so they can provide well-informed advice to those who are suffering, usually in silence, loneliness, and fear. Spiritual and mental health knowledge like what you'll find in these pages can increase compassion in the church for those who are like the lost lambs that Jesus described. They need a place to be, and someone to be with them. This book will inform, inspire, and equip you to fulfill this special calling.

~ David B. Biebel, DMin
Healthy Life Press

Foreword

As a book division consultant, I reviewed and approved the publication of the first edition of this book in 2000. Little did I know that it would find its way to a church in Paris, a small hospital library in Niger, a coffee table in Japan, or to Taiwan in a Chinese version. In all these settings, it proved to be a source of mental health education for many sufferers of anxiety and for those who care for and love them. I also did not predict its employment in the September 11 tragedy in New York, acknowledged in a communication from first lady, Laura Bush. Moreover, it has served as a training text for countless students in pastoral and mental health counseling and audiences concerned about psychological health.

This new version of the book contains valuable updates from the *Diagnostic and Statistical Manual of Mental Health Disorders, 5th Edition* (May 2013, American Psychiatric Press). Brand-new chapters on the treatment of a fictional patient are included to describe the steps of cognitive behavioral therapy (CBT), a well-researched effective clinical tool. The book retains its use of diagnostic criteria, illustrative narratives, pragmatic solutions, resources, and medical information to aid in the recognition and care of conditions that cause excessive worrying. Provocatively inspirational is the chapter on "The Word of God," lending credence to the integration of Scripture into CBT.

In my work as a physician and professor at Duke University Medical Center, and as director of Duke's Center for Spirituality, Theology, and Health, I have championed the goal of educating the Christian (and world) community in the area of mental health education, and have conducted research on integrating religious faith into counseling with patients who have the kinds of problems that this book addresses. I believe that this updated version of Dr. Eng's classic book will be a source of comfort, hope, and knowledge to many, including those who struggle with anxiety and those who wish to help.

I applaud her creation of another life-changing book that will be a long-sought-for oasis of relief and peace.

~ Harold G. Koenig, MD
Professor of Psychiatry & Behavioral Sciences
Associate Professor of Medicine
Director, Center for Spirituality, Theology and Health
Duke University Medical Center, Durham, North Carolina
Distinguished Adjunct Professor
King Abdulaziz University, Jeddah, Saudi Arabia

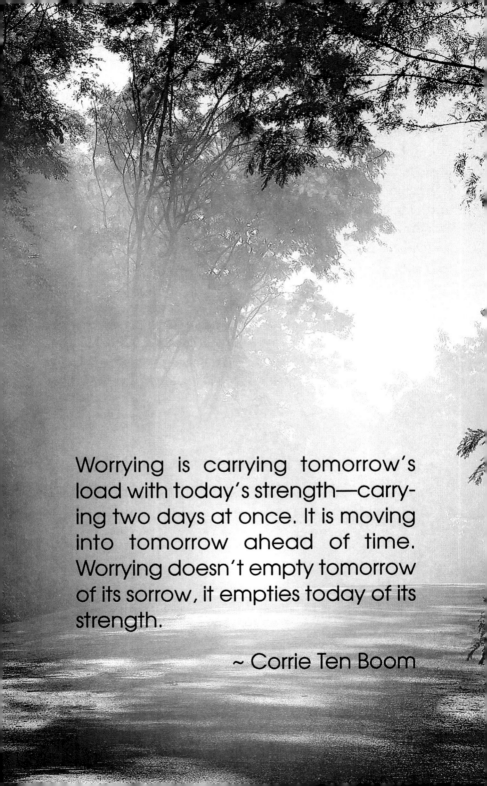

Worrying is carrying tomorrow's load with today's strength—carrying two days at once. It is moving into tomorrow ahead of time. Worrying doesn't empty tomorrow of its sorrow, it empties today of its strength.

~ Corrie Ten Boom

CHAPTER 1

Introduction

*T*HE IMPETUS FOR THIS BOOK COME FROM CLINICAL EXPERIENCE with many patients who resemble the biblical figure Martha. She, by virtue of her faith, hard work, and hospitality was a pillar of an early religious community in Bethany. Modern day sufferers of anxiety, with excellent track records of performance in their church, can become derailed and filled with worry. Negotiating this turn of events is not only an important task for the individual, but it is ultimately shared with the church. This book was written to equip those concerned with the restoration of these faithful, talented individuals.

The description of Martha's worried state is depicted in Luke 10:38-42:

> *As Jesus and his disciples were on their way, he came to a village where a woman named Martha opened her home to him. She had a sister named Mary, who sat at the Lord's feet listening to what he*

was saying. But Martha was distracted by all the preparations that had to be made. She came to him and asked, "Lord, don't you care that my sister has left me to do the work by myself? Tell her to help me!" "Martha, Martha," the Lord answered, "You're worried and upset about many things, but only one thing is needed, Mary has chosen what is better, and it will not be taken away from her."

Martha is worried and upset about many things. Her worries began after she extended an invitation to the Lord to come to her house, which she appeared to do wholeheartedly. However, anxiety took hold and instead of sitting at the Lord's feet she became distracted about the preparations and worried about much. The Lord indicates that Mary has chosen what is better, implying that Martha had the same choice. Based on this brief dialogue it is clear that to worry or not to worry is often a choice.

Many would follow the counsel of the apostle Paul found in Philippians 4:6, "Do not be anxious about anything, but in everything, by prayer and petition, with thanksgiving, present your requests to God." However, at times, people have difficulty heeding this Scripture despite its authenticity and genuineness.

Living in this age of anxiety, there may be many reasons why people worry. Real life stresses impact our lives. Yet worry in its most overshadowing and consuming form does not yield any benefits. It is in this context that one should claim the choice, choosing not to worry versus choosing to worry. How can one make the choice?

There are multiple ways. Mary, in the gospel account, chose to sit at the Lord's feet and listen to His teachings. This is a time-honored method and proven to be an effective anxiety-relieving strategy for many. Some people may have to deal with psychological reasons for their anxiety, such as personal conflicts or learned misperceptions of the world. This makes it difficult for them to "sit down at the Lord's feet" and simply listen. Martha's worries and distractions prevented her from listening to Jesus in a receptive manner.

Some causes of anxiety may not be as easy to discern. For example, some may be suffering from a medical condition in which anxiety is a prominent feature. This is true in the church setting as well as in society at large. All these people require the sensitive help of family, friends, ministers, educational resources, books, or professional counseling.

It is my hope that this book will help you identify, understand, and help those within your community who are struggling with anxiety. It contains the narratives of fictional composites of potentially real people. This manner of illustration is designed to improve your recognition of people afflicted with anxiety disorders. These are conditions in which fear and anxiety have gone haywire. Ordinarily, fear and anxiety are normal human responses to threatening situations, preparing a person for fight or flight. Fear can also sharpen a person for action and is in many cases adaptive. These natural human responses are not abnormal.

People worry for many reasons
Real life stresses impact our lives.
Yet worry in its most overshadowing and consuming form does not yield any benefits.

Anxiety disorders, by contrast, are marked by anxiety gone awry. The chapters on depression, post-traumatic stress disorder, obsessive compulsive disorder, and premenstrual dysphoric disorder are included because many people who suffer from these problems may have anxiety as their main complaint.

Most of the narratives describe the sufferer but some are written in the first person, from the point of view of a fellow church member or friend, in an attempt to draw the reader into the predicaments experienced by those suffering with anxiety disorders. A certain amount of discomfort will have to be tolerated by the reader in order to learn from the text. In a community and a society where mental health issues tend to be misunderstood, stigmatized, and avoided, tolerating the tension may be no simple request. However, it is worthwhile to persevere and learn in order to help, in part because these are often people who not only have the capacity to function, but are the "doers," if not the pillars of the church or organization.

These men and women need to be appreciated for their significant contributions because they often carry on very useful lives at home or at work. But at times this is disrupted when they are plagued with worries caused by their condition. Unfortunately, it may also interfere with their relationships at home, work, or in the organizations in which they serve. Recognizing these individuals and helping to care for them will ultimately help the entire group of which they are a part. Their problems are real. Understanding the psychiatric causes of severe anxiety will help other leaders, counselors, students, or caring individuals to have a keener understanding and sensitivity toward the "Marthas" all around them. They will also learn to discern when sufferers need to obtain care from a mental health professional.

This book is an educational tool. Readers should not try to make diagnostic judgments or treatment plans on the basis of this text. My intention is to broaden the reader's understanding of the psychiatric factors causing anxiety, which is a neglected topic in many religious libraries. In my work, I have helped many anxious patients resume serving the Lord. The goal of this book is to help you learn to do the same.

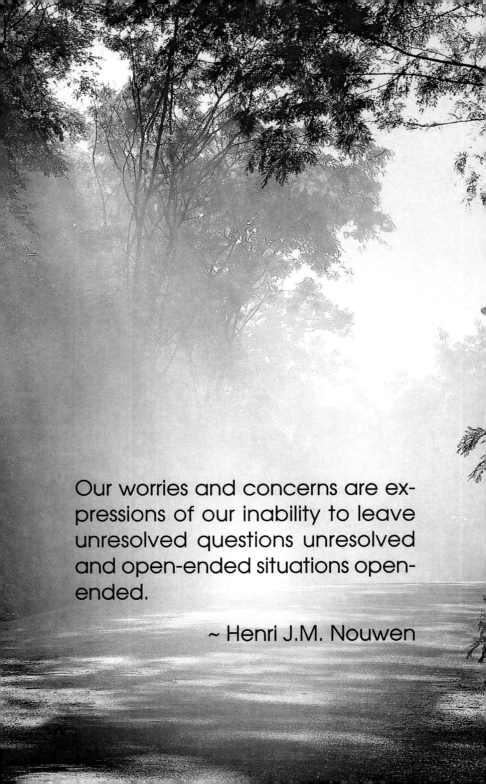

Our worries and concerns are expressions of our inability to leave unresolved questions unresolved and open-ended situations open-ended.

~ Henri J.M. Nouwen

CHAPTER 2

Panic
"The Oppressor"

KIM, A YOUNG PASTOR TRAINED IN KOREA, WAS INVITED TO come to the United States to continue his work among the churches in a large city. A gifted speaker, he was extremely dedicated to his work, preparing for his sermons in a methodical and thorough manner. He was well received by the churches that he visited, and people often looked forward to the times when he would deliver the message. Kim was delighted about his successful speaking engagements in the United States despite the fact that at times he was anxious about different aspects of life in his new environment.

About the wintertime of his first year in this country, Kim began to experience a strange sense of foreboding. Each time as he was preparing for a sermon he became quite nervous and occasionally felt that he was paralyzed and unable to function. Quite often, out of the blue, he would experience episodes of intense anxiety, sweating, and feelings of impending doom as his heart pounded furiously. Kim attributed these attacks to "spiritual oppression" as he felt that these attacks were designed to impede his work in preaching. He found comfort in prayer and meditation, and continued to persevere in his work. He shared some of his problems with senior pastors in various churches, and they all acknowledged that the work of the ministry can be at times stressful and met with opposition. They all shared their experiences with Kim and encouraged him and prayed for him. He derived a sense of comfort from this support.

Kim's symptoms began to worsen throughout that winter and into the early spring. These attacks became more frequent and occurred regularly, as much as three times a day. They were sudden and came without warning, but at times Kim did notice that they would be triggered by his preparation for a sermon. He called this thing "the monster." He fought furiously to ignore the symptoms and remain calm, in order to persevere with his work. He decided that a visit to the doctor might be helpful so he made an appointment with a local internist. He was reassured that his entire physical exam was normal, and he was proclaimed to be in a "good state of health."

"The monster" continued to afflict Kim. He longed to return to his homeland where he thought he might regain his peace of mind. His mental turmoil and grueling schedule had been very draining. How he longed to truly rest. His mind, which was at the height of unrest, began to dwell on these recurrent attacks and whether or not he would be able to function as a minister. He lived in fear of the "monster's" approach and presence. True, he could distract himself by prayer, taking long walks, and participating in fellowship with his church members. However, the distractions did not last very long and soon he would begin worrying again. He found himself avoiding people and places where he would not be able to escape, should the "monster" attack him there. The worry began to turn into despair. Finally, one spring day, he sat down at his desk to write his letter of resignation to his pastor.

Dear Reverend,

I know that in the work of the Lord there is persecution and opposition from the enemy, and alas, I think that my troubles have been from such a cause. But I find that I am in such a weakened state that my faith, which I thought had no bounds, is really minuscule in size. I find that it does not sustain me to do the work that I've been called to do; therefore, I am most saddened by having to write this letter of resignation. It seems that this thing that I call the "monster" leaves me intensely fearful and shaken and has affected my ability to work. It haunts me daily. It causes me to avoid the very people whom I long to serve. I could no longer in good conscience preach from the pulpit towards a goal of strengthening the congregation when I now cower in fear when alone in my room. My hope is to return to Korea and from that point I do not know what the future holds. I am sorry to do this because I really don't wish to leave this work, which I wished my whole life to do. Under the circumstances I find that there is no other recourse.

Respectfully,
Kim

When the senior pastor read this letter, he closed his eyes and reflected on Kim's ministry in the United States. What a shame that this gifted young man would have to abandon his work because of this affliction. And what was this affliction? The senior pastor, who was not used to not having answers, began to ponder. Is this a spiritual oppression of the "enemy?" Is this the manifestation of an overly stressed mind? Could this be the symptom of a yet undiagnosed medical illness? He felt quite helpless at discovering the explanation. But he was convinced that an answer must be obtained and that Kim should not have to give up his brilliant work because of this undefined, inexplicable problem. *What should I do?* he asked himself.

Discussion

Kim is suffering from a classic case of panic disorder. Panic attacks are episodes of intense anxiety that often develop "out-of-the-blue." They are characterized by physical symptoms such as sweating, heart palpitations, flushing, "a sensation of knots in the stomach," shakiness, dizziness, and other symptoms that often accompany anxiety. In addition, when one is experiencing a panic attack, one's thoughts usually resemble the following: *Something terrible is going to happen to me* or *I am losing my mind.* These are called thoughts of impending doom. Often, people attribute these symptoms to a physical condition. As a result they may make frequent trips to the doctor or the hospital emergency room only to learn each time that they have a clean bill of health. For some it seems easier to attribute their symptoms to an underlying physical illness rather than to something that is more psychological in origin.

Many problems may result from panic attacks. When the attacks reach a certain frequency or cause

If you have learned to automatically give the most negative attribution to every situation, you will no doubt be constantly anxious.

significant anticipation of future attacks, we call this condition panic disorder. People often live in fear of having a panic attack once they experience their first one.

Many refer to their panic attacks with terms like "the monster" because of their suddenness, intensity, and unpredictability. They truly feel as if they are plagued or even stalked by a monster. Patients have described panic attacks as "a monkey on my back," "a green monster waiting to pounce," or a "shadowy figure lurking behind." Among Christians, another common conceptualization of a panic attack is that it represents "spiritual oppression;" in other words, the causative agent is a demon oppressor.

In Kim's case, having found no medical reason for his attacks and not recognizing this problem as that of an anxiety disorder, Kim's conclusion was that it represented a spiritual attack from the enemy. This formulation was not accurate in Kim's case. Recognizing that this was a classic case of panic disorder might have led him to seek appropriate treatment. According to Dr. Jerrold Rosenbaum, of the Department of Psychiatry at Harvard Medical School, ". . . the key to effective treatment of panic disorder is early recognition of the condition. . . . Early referral to a psychiatrist or a psychologist can be cost-effective in the long run."[1] Detection and treatment would not only relieve the anxiety symptoms, but would have allowed Kim to stay and continue the important work that he was doing in the United States. In addition, he might have had a different perspective on his faith, which he branded to be poor in his resignation letter.

There are effective treatments for panic disorder. These would include psychological therapies such as cognitive behavioral therapy (CBT) designed for individuals and groups who suffer from panic disorder. CBT is a form of "talking therapy" in which certain automatic, anxiety-provoking thoughts are identified and corrected. For example, if a rod-like structure is held to your head and you believe it to be a gun, then you will be highly anxious. On the other hand, if you believe it to be a pen, then you will remain calm. The point is that people's perception of a given situation governs their mood. If they have learned to automatically give the most negative attribution to every situation, they will no doubt be constantly anxious. Often these thoughts are irrational, unrealistic, and catastrophic, and in the case of the Christian believer, they are usually not biblical. It is, therefore, important in therapy to unlearn old patterns of thinking and learn to restructure one's appraisal of reality. Automatic, catastrophic thoughts are contradicted by Scripture such as Jeremiah 29:11, "For I know the plans I have for you," declares the LORD, "plans to prosper you and not to harm you, plans to give you hope and a future." In therapy, the Christian can learn to use individualized, biblically-based as well as other realistic, positive thoughts to replace his anxiety provoking ones.

Relaxation techniques are used to relieve the physical tension produced in panic disorder. During relaxation, the person is asked to focus on and relax muscle groups in a systematic way. For example, he may start by relaxing the hand and arm muscles, followed by the facial, chest, abdominal, and leg muscles. He may be asked to visualize a relaxing scene, such as a sandy beach on a beautiful day. By practicing these techniques daily, the person learns how to gain control over his body and decrease physical tension.

The other major element of CBT addresses behavior. People suffering from panic disorder may begin to develop avoidance behaviors, such as refraining from entering public places or from traveling beyond a "safety zone" for fear of having a panic attack. This condition, called agoraphobia, may culminate in the worst case scenario where a person is homebound. It takes significant personal motivation to overcome agoraphobia. Individuals with this condition must take gradual steps toward once again traveling outside the home. Such steps will produce some anxiety, which must be tolerated. Persistence will eventually lead to venturing out with more ease, a process called habituation. Homework assignments are designed in the therapy to practice exposure to feared places according to an individualized hierarchy.

Avoidance behaviors are discouraged as they lead to further restrictions and limitations in function. As the person ventures into feared places and maintains a consistent pattern of doing so, he will gradually become less anxious. He can also substitute his unrealistic, catastrophic thoughts with more calming ones. For example: *There is no evidence that going into this restaurant has the power to cause a panic attack,* versus *What if I have a panic attack at this restaurant?* "What if . . ." statements frequently plague the thinking of anxious people. Often the "what if..." thought represents the worst possible case scenario. In addition, the likelihood of that scenario occurring is highly overestimated in the mind of the anxious person. Managing the "what ifs . . ." with objectivity and discarding them as highly unlikely can counteract this tendency.

Many people with panic disorder misinterpret normal bodily sensations as abnormal and as a sign of a medical emergency. Sensations such as a rapid heart rate in response to heat, anger, excitement, and exercise are mistakenly perceived as a sign of a heart problem or the beginnings of a panic attack. This misinterpretation alone may generate sufficient anxiety to fuel a panic attack. Stopping the vicious cycle at the very beginning by saying to oneself that the heart normally beats faster under certain conditions and that this response is characteristic of a well-functioning cardiac system will thwart the rise in anxiety. For some reason, anxious people are more keenly sensitive to bodily sensations of which most people are unaware. Correcting their tendency to misinterpret these sensations can be extremely therapeutic.

A host of medications have been found to be effective in ameliorating the symptoms of panic. These medications—called selective serotonin reuptake inhibitors (SSRIs)—such as citalopram, sertraline, fluoxetine, and others are also used to treat depression. Many people complaining of panic attacks may be suffering from depression as well. Hence, treating them with antidepressants that also relieve panic attacks serves a double purpose. Proper psychiatric evaluations of people suffering from panic disorder would determine the appropriate medication.

Treatment may involve psychotherapy alone or a combination of psychotherapy and medication. It is worth mentioning that medical conditions mimicking panic disorder should be considered and ruled out. Common conditions mimicking panic disorder include thyroid disease, cardiac problems such as arrhythmias, respiratory diseases, tumors of the adrenal gland, inner ear problems, seizures, overactive parathyroid glands, and many others. Hence, it is vital to obtain a medical evaluation for patients suffering anxiety to make sure they do not have an "anxiety disorder due to another medical condition."[2]

> For some with panic disorder, it seems easier to attribute their symptoms to an underlying physical illness rather than to something that is more psychological in origin.

Anxiety is seen in response to substance abuse and a side effect of many medications. Symptoms may occur either during the period of intoxication or while withdrawing. This condition is called "substance/medication-induced anxiety disorder."[3] Classes of drugs which can cause panic attacks and anxiety include methylpheni-date, cocaine, phencyclidine, hallucinogens, and excessive use of caffeine. Withdrawing from certain drugs or medications can produce anxiety. Such drugs include narcotics, tranquilizers (benzodiazepines), alcohol, barbiturates, and others. Certain medications that produce side effects of anxiety include antihistamines, steroids, insulin, thyroid hormones, asthma medications, oral contraceptives, and some medicines for Parkinson's disease.[4] A thorough psychiatric evaluation, drug screening, and medical check-up would distinguish whether anxiety or panic is cause by a substance, medication, or another medical condition. A detailed history might identify other family members with similar symptoms.

Kim's life might have changed with early recognition and intervention. Early intervention might have helped him and those around him. Because this form of anxiety can lead to demoralization and depression, one needs to seek help as soon as possible.

How People Can Help

You can help those who suffer from panic disorder. The following suggestions include some pragmatic as well as theoretical considerations for professionals, family, and friends:

1. Naturally, spiritual health is the expertise of the trained clergy, but in the situation of anxiety symptoms and particularly in panic disorder, it is crucial not to overlook the physical health of the individual. This is because the anxiety may be a symptom of a hidden physical or medical condition, which must be detected in order to properly help the person. Therefore, the minister should inquire about the person's physical health and whether or not he has consulted a physician. If the person has not sought any medical attention for his or her panic attacks, the minister can urge him to do so.

   The sufferer often gratefully receives such a recommendation. His anxiety may be reduced by the suggestion of a medical basis for the condition. Most likely, the sufferer has been gripped by many unanswered questions about the oppressive panic attacks. Further, this recommendation from a trusted spiritual advisor represents "permission" to approach the problem from other than a purely spiritual direction, reassuring the sufferer that the minister is interested in his total health and not quick to couch everything exclusively in spiritual terms.

Once the internist or the family doctor does the medical evaluation, there are two possible outcomes. One is that the doctor has identified a medical illness causing panic attacks, and the appropriate treatment is initiated. The other, which is quite common, is that the sufferer receives a clean bill of health, in which case the doctor may make a referral to a mental health professional, be it a psychiatrist, psychologist, or therapist.

The sufferer may need help in following through on the referral. There may be many issues that make it difficult for him or her to obtain mental health care. Many of these issues relate to false ideas about having a mental problem and the stigma that is prevalent in society and even in the church. Going for mental health care may represent a substantial blow to self-esteem. A caring individual can show support for this action and reframe it in a positive way; such as, "I'm thankful you've been able to find help, and in my opinion the most reasonable approach is to make the best use of it, so I'm with you all the way."

2. The sufferer may need help finding appropriate mental health care, particularly if the person continues to suffer acutely from the panic attacks. The

majority of people with panic disorder in this country benefit from either cognitive-behavioral psychotherapy, medications, or in most cases a combination of both. With that in mind, one should try to find treatment where both modalities are offered, such as a psychiatrist with expertise in the cognitive-behavioral treatment of panic disorder, a therapist who works closely with a psychiatrist dispensing medications, or anxiety disorder programs which staff a team that provides the different modalities of treatment. Helping someone find the best source of treatment from the start can substantially reduce the possibility of future complications of anxiety.

3. A caring individual or minister should learn as much as he or she can about panic disorder. Having a clear understanding about the illness provides a sense of the potential severity of the attacks and how frightening and incapacitating they can be. Psychoeducation—the education of the patient, family members, and other involved individuals—has become an important element of therapy for panic disorder.

Understanding the topic of risk versus benefit, when it comes to the use of medication in treating panic disorder, is crucial. When medications are considered in treatment, the psychiatrist or other physician will discuss the pros and cons of a particular drug and what is expected from its use. Each of the different drugs in the treatment of panic disorder has its own benefits and side effects.

Literature summarizing these points may be provided by the treatment provider. Only after the patient has been reasonably informed and has discussed all options with the doctor, including what is to be expected if no medication is taken, can any patient decide whether or not she wants to take the drug. With the patient's permission, a caring individual may be part of this interchange, being sure the patient understands all options and reasonable results, as well as prescription details as appropriate.

Caring individuals can learn a great deal by listening and supporting the sufferer's decision making process. They should try to understand what the sufferer is willing to tolerate in light of the clear benefits of the medication being considered. The doctor should describe serious negative side effects and risks with the patient. The patient should understand that he or she is the primary person responsible for monitoring for serious consequences or side effects, because if these occur, then the patient should contact the doctor immediately.

At this juncture, it is important that the patient feels understood and also understands the variables and is able to make a decision that he believes to be best for his life at the current time.

Many patients who suffer from panic disorder benefit from books written on the subject. Authors who have gone through the illness and the process of treatment generally write these. Some are written by experts in the field writing to a general audience. See the resource chapter at the end of the book.

How the Integration of Theology and Psychology Can Help

To conclude this chapter on panic disorder and how to help, it is worthwhile to underscore some aspects of the integration of theology and psychology. While these can remain separate universes of discourse for most people, integration of the two areas may provide a great benefit for the minister trying to help a congregant. It is unfortunate when proponents in each of these areas view each other with suspicion and at times overt hostility. Where possible, a minister should have a conceptual framework that embodies the truth from religious beliefs integrated with models of psychological concepts. This can be most beneficial to the person suffering from anxiety.

For example, take the concept of fear. The Christian community has understood at least two sides to fear. There is the good fear embodied in the notion of "the fear of the Lord" (Proverbs 9:10) which emphasizes that believers need a genuine, reverential trust in God in order to negotiate life wisely and successfully. Biblical support for this can be found in Psalm 115:11:

Pastors have the platform to advise and encourage their people to overcome their negative fears while at the same time fostering a reverential healthy fear of God.

"You who fear him, trust in the Lord—he is their help and shield."

By contrast, the negative side of fear describes a fearful and timid spirit, which prevents a believer from doing what God wants from him or her. Moses expressed his fear of leading God's people out of Egypt, claiming that he lacked the capacity to be an effective leader. This type of fear limits believers from doing what is either their responsibility, goal, or mission. Scripture provides clarification on this aspect of fear in 2 Timothy 1:7, "For God hath not given us the spirit of fear; but of power, and of love, and of a sound mind" (KJV). Ministers are quite familiar with these two aspects of fear and countless sermons and biblical texts can be used to define and illustrate these two divergent expressions of fear. Moreover, pastors advise and encourage their people to overcome their negative fears while at the same time fostering a reverential healthy fear of God.

There are also two sides to psychological fear. Fear can alert the individual to fight or flee in a dangerous situation. It signals the body to act to preserve the life and welfare of a person in danger. Fear sets off an alarm system that mobilizes the body by creating the optimum physiological conditions for action. The heart races to pump blood to all the muscles, breathing is more rapid to deliver oxygen to the body, and there is an outpouring of adrenaline. This is healthy fear, which is necessary for the protection of the body. It might operate when a person walks down an alley in a dangerous neighborhood, is approached by an assailant, or being stalked by a wild animal.

On a lesser scale, a healthy fear or anxiety can motivate a person to study well for a test or to be psychologically prepared for an interview. This healthy, adaptive fear is contrasted with crippling or negative fear. The fear in panic disorder is imagined and unrealistic, but nonetheless terrifying, as if the "monster" were real. The resulting paralyzing false alarm rings throughout the brain and body, serving no adaptive function while leaving exhaustion in its wake.

The two sided conceptualization of theological fear and psychological fear is but one example of biblical analogies which approximate secular ones. When taught to patients, this concept can create a deeper sense of understanding about their illness because it integrates the two worlds in which they dwell—the heart and mind.

There are many other examples of integrative work, a topic that is beyond the scope of this book. However, in clinical situations, many patients respond well when an attempt is made to integrate theology and psychology. After all, this is what they are trying to do when they are coping with their illness. A minister or even a caring individual attuned to the value of this integration can provide much insight and support to an anxious individual. When a person is in the midst of struggling with mental illness, it is far better to identify helpful tools from religion and psychology, possibly including medicine, than to polarize these disciplines.

Recall how Kim obtained comfort and support from his meeting with other pastors during his difficult time. The therapeutic elements of such meetings are the hallmarks of Christian support, including prayer and scriptural sustenance. Can one quantify the therapeutic value of knowing that one's fears and needs are being uplifted in prayer? Given the Christian's belief system, the contribution must indeed be significant. Scriptural sustenance, when used appropriately, is another tool that can be utilized from the realm of theology to assist in a psychological problem. A psychologist, therapist, or psychiatrist would do well to acknowledge how much the church community and its inherent assets have contributed to the progress of their clients and patients. More research and education should be developed in integrating psychology and religion, not merely on a theoretical basis but in a pragmatic framework designed to assist patients.

Fear in the midst of the storm is instinctive and beneficial. Fear of a storm that could happen is not. It's an intrusive emotion that can lead us to a greatly diminished life.

~ David Jeremiah

CHAPTER 3

A Treatment Described

NANCY, A THIRTY-THREE-YEAR-OLD MARRIED WOMAN, EXPERIenced her first panic attack while watching a Disney movie with her children at the local theater. Gripped by a sudden onset of sweating, palpitations, and shortness of breath accompanied by an intense fear of dying, she rushed out of the building with her confused youngsters. Her husband drove her to the hospital emergency room where the doctors did a complete medical evaluation, the results of which were all normal to Nancy's surprise. The next day she visited her family doctor who also gave her a clean bill of health. He learned that, although Nancy never had experienced this before, her mother had suffered from anxiety and depression many years earlier and had been treated with medications. He suggested that Nancy may also be suffering from anxiety and recommended professional counseling. Although Nancy was not convinced that this was merely anxiety, she complied with her doctor and made an appointment with a therapist for the following week. In the meantime, she feared that she would have another attack and in fact had two more episodes of palpitations and sweating while driving her children to school and while resting at home on the weekend. This last episode worried her so much that she begged her husband to bring her to the emergency room. Again, the medical evaluation proved to be completely normal, including blood tests and an EKG that showed her heart to be in good condition.

Discussion

Nancy's condition would usually be treated by addressing the person's automatic, unrealistic, and catastrophic thoughts that trigger anxiety. Often the sufferer does not recognize having these thoughts. The patient is instructed to monitor for unrealistic worries, which often begin with the words "what if." The patient keeps a journal of all anxiety episodes, writing down these thoughts when they occur. The journal includes her rating the anxiety on a scale of 1 to 10 with one being calm and 10 being the highest. It should describe what was going on when the attack occurred, how the patient tried to quell the anxiety, and a re-rating of the anxiety after such measures.

Psychoeducation about panic disorder is done throughout the treatment (see previous chapter for facts about panic disorder). The following excerpts from Nancy's journal were the focus of her work with her therapist in their subsequent sessions:

#1—Sunday

I (Nancy) was in church and wanted to take my usual aisle seat. But it was crowded that day and all the aisle seats were taken. My children asked if we could sit in the middle of a pew next to their friends. As I approached my seat, I began to feel anxious and dizzy and my heart started to palpitate. My thought was "What if I had a panic attack?" Seated in the middle of the aisle instead of the end made me more anxious because I would not be able to escape easily. I rated the anxiety a "5." I tried to talk to my children, but everything seemed so unreal. It took a while, but eventually my anxiety came down to a "3" after I began to focus on the speaker.

Treatment

The therapist questions Nancy about her thoughts just prior to the anxiety symptoms, which occurred when her children asked to sit in the middle of the pew. She thinks a moment and says, "I do not think I had other thoughts." But the therapist presses gently and Nancy realizes that she

> Often the sufferer does not recognize having automatic, unrealistic, and catastrophic thoughts that trigger anxiety. A journal can help such a person gain insight into this pattern.

had thoughts of running out of the seat, pushing against all the others and appearing "crazy" as she rushes out of the church. When asked if she has ever done anything like that before, she says "no." The therapist asks Nancy, "What is the likelihood this will happen?" Nancy, thinks again and says "Probably never, but I'm afraid that it might." More education is done indicating that in panic disorder, the fear seems real but statistically what is feared is unlikely to happen.

#2—Wednesday

I kept thinking that there must be something wrong with my health. I was checking the Internet on the topic of heart attacks and strokes because when I feel dizzy and my heart beats wildly, it seems just like the list of symptoms of a heart attack. As I was reading about this, I became anxious up to a "6." I know my internist did an EKG and physical exam and everything was normal. Even the two times I went to the emergency room, I was told that everything was alright with my heart. I tried to calm down by telling myself that my doctor and the E.R. could not be wrong, and then turned on some music. I think my anxiety went down to a "3."

Treatment

Many patients suffering from panic disorder do an excessive amount of checking on their physical health via the Internet, books, and consultation with friends or health professionals to alleviate their fears. The therapist conveys this to Nancy and states that frequent checking actually worsens the anxiety by causing her to dwell on her unrealistic thoughts. This creates a "worry loop" by aggravating the anxiety, and should be stopped. Stopping this activity seems counterintuitive to many patients as they hope to solve the problem by doing the research. Nancy is reminded that this is similar to introducing the "what if..." thoughts into her mind over and over again. In the session, the therapist points out that Nancy has begun to use the coping skill of realistic appraisal of her health by telling herself that evaluations by her doctor and two E.R. visits could not possibly be wrong. She has restructured her thoughts by believing that a normal EKG and other tests demonstrated that she did not have a heart attack or a stroke. The therapist then points out that a measureable decrease in her anxiety rating shows that correcting her thoughts is indeed effective in reducing anxiety. Nancy is shown that she has control over her anxiety, a fact unrecognized by her previously. Nancy and the therapist end the session with the assignment to continue journaling any episodes of heightened anxiety or panic for the next week.

#1—Monday

I was standing in line at the bank. The line was rather long but I had to take care of my bank statement that day or a check would bounce. Suddenly, I became very anxious and dizzy and short of breath. I wanted to leave the bank immediately because I was afraid I would pass out. The anxiety was a "9." I forced myself to stay, but I don't know how I did it.

Treatment

First, the therapist congratulates Nancy on staying in line at the bank despite her anxiety, as this is crucial to developing coping skills. Nancy is asked to remember her thoughts, even though she does not know how she remained in line. Nancy remembers that the exit was close to several desks occupied by customers filling out their bank slips. She feared she would run out and bump into them causing a scene. Frightened by this thought, she quickly reasoned that she has exited the bank many times without any difficulty. Therefore this must be a "what if" thought, so she had used a thought stopping technique of visualizing a "red stop sign." She then refocused on her deposit slips for the bank teller and noted some relief. Even though it seemed like a long time, she finally heard the teller call for her. Again, the therapist congratulates her and points out how much progress she is making in monitoring her catastrophic thoughts and using her coping skills to stop them.

#2—Sunday

This past Sunday was Mother's day. We went to church and everything went well. Later in the afternoon, I was reading my cards when suddenly my heart was pounding and I was very anxious. My anxiety reached a "6." I told myself that this was only anxiety and there was nothing wrong with me physically. Even though my heart continued to pound for a while, I was able to reduce my anxiety to a "3." In the past, I would have run to the emergency room or called my doctor, but I realized that what I had was anxiety and I remembered that you told me it would not kill me. It was then that I noted that my anxiety went down to a "3" from the original rating of "6." I still did not like that uncomfortable feeling of being "keyed up," which lasted several hours.

Treatment

The therapist asks Nancy what she was thinking at the time of the panic and how she had quelled the anxiety. Nancy denies any "what if" thoughts, indicating how happy she was celebrating Mother's Day with her family at church. She did use the intervention of imagining a calm, beautiful beach scene (visual imagery), and breathing regularly while relaxing her abdominal muscles. Later, Nancy tells the therapist that she had eaten chocolates received for Mother's Day. This offers the therapist an opportunity to teach Nancy about caffeine. Panic disorder patients are particularly sensitive to the stimulating effects of caffeine, which produces the side effect of anxiety and panic. While this does not occur in non-sufferers, even small or ordinary consumption of caffeine-containing substances can precipitate anxiety in patients like Nancy. Nancy is given a list of items that contain caffeine or other stimulants: coffee, tea, chocolate, certain types of sodas, many over the counter cold and allergy medications, dental injections containing epinephrine, and a number of prescription medications. Nancy should alert her physicians and dentist about her sensitivity to caffeine and stimulants.

#3—Thursday

I was riding the train to work at the part-time job I have

done for fifteen years. I remember proofreading a report that I had to write for my boss when suddenly I felt nervous. Then I became lightheaded and dizzy and felt something terrible was going to happen to me. I tried to think about my thoughts and what got me nervous. I rated my anxiety a "5." I think I was worried that my boss would not like my report.

Treatment

The therapist asks Nancy about further thoughts, then she reveals: "If my boss did not like my report, then I would feel that 'I am a failure.'" In an effort to provide Nancy a more realistic appraisal, the therapist inquires about her boss's satisfaction with her work for the past fifteen years.

A life-long struggle to meet unreasonable expectations can be the true basis for one's perceived inability to measure up in the present situation, whether at work or at home.

Nancy indicates her boss has been very pleased with her work and has never given her a negative review. In fact, Nancy cannot find any evidence for her automatic, negative self-statement, "I'm a failure," or its equivalent, "I'm not good enough." These are identified by the therapist as unrealistic thoughts that need to be monitored, for they can lead to feelings of anxiety or sadness.

Nancy states,

"My dad used to make me feel that way. Every time I brought home a report card or any test, he would always complain that I didn't do well enough to meet his standards." The therapist acknowledges that this may be the place where Nancy learned her negative self-statements, but again encourages her to do a realistic appraisal of the truth, especially in her current life. Nancy concludes, "My boss respects what I do and it's not likely that he would criticize my report. I know God has blessed me with a good job and a good relationship with my boss." She admits, "I don't understand why I worry so much. Sometimes I think that God will see me as a failure, too."

Treatment

Here, the therapist reinforces the same coping tools to help Nancy restructure this negative appraisal of her relationship with God. A keen understanding of Nancy's faith and biblical beliefs adds great value to the treatment. A subsequent chapter entitled "The Word of God" will shed light on these beliefs.

But to conclude this chapter, let's look at a couple more of Nancy's journal entries and treatment.

Nancy's Additional Journal Entry #1

The other day I was rushing around getting ready for work. I did not have to hurry as I had ample time, but I felt as if I was going to be late. I began to be a little short of breath but I told myself it was just anxiety. What should I do when this happens?

Treatment

The therapist and Nancy identified the unrealistic cognition driving the anxiety, as "What if I'm late?" Nancy recognized that the shortness of breath was due to anxiety but did not know the thought behind it. Once identified, Nancy observed how often she would rush unnecessarily before leaving the house.

Psychoeducation here involves informing Nancy that many

anxious people have a distorted sense of time available to them; their rushing to get things accomplished in what is perceived as too short a period of time leads to symptoms. Teaching patients to slow down, even to the point of deliberate "robotic" movement and telling oneself the truth about the plentiful time available will help relieve the anxiety.

Nancy's Additional Journal Entry #2

I haven't had any full-blown panic attacks this week, but I feel constantly physically tense. I notice this especially when I am doing nothing or just watching TV. At night, this muscle tension occasionally makes it hard to sleep. What should I do?

Treatment

The therapist teaches Nancy some relaxation exercises, helping her to focus on a relaxed, normal pattern of breathing while expanding and loosening the abdominal muscles, which she should practice on a regular basis. The therapist asks Nancy what her favorite, relaxing scene would be and suggests that she imagine that she is there for ten minutes at a time. Finally, "Progressive Muscle Relaxation,"[1] is introduced, teaching Nancy to focus on each of the following muscle groups and intentionally relaxing them—the hands, arms, facial muscles, chest muscles, abdomen, and legs. This technique is further elaborated in the work of this therapy's founder Dr. Edmund Jacobson.

Other relaxation exercises are available and Nancy should be encouraged to find those that work for her. She should be advised to practice what she has learned in the session daily, if possible, so it becomes automatic. First she should choose quiet, calm times to practice and then she should graduate to times of tension or anxiety. These are excellent additions to her collection of coping skills.

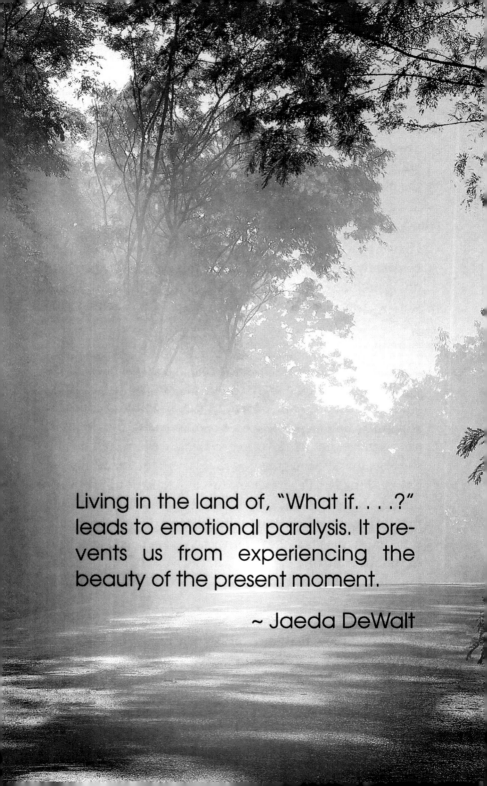

Living in the land of, "What if. . . .?"
leads to emotional paralysis. It prevents us from experiencing the
beauty of the present moment.

~ Jaeda DeWalt

CHAPTER 4

Social Anxiety Disorder
"A Loss for Words"

ELICIA, A NURSE IN THE LOCAL COMMUNITY HOSPITAL, DID HER job excellently. She was praised for her competent nursing care, her compassion, and her dedication to the service of others. She was active in her local church and participated in many of the women's meetings. Because of her character and her hard work, she was promoted at her job. Part of the requirement of her new status was to teach large groups of nurses in her local community. She was exhilarated by the promotion but quickly became anxious because her new responsibilities required her to speak publicly.

As a child she was always shy and inhibited. It was with great difficulty that she separated from her mother in order to go to her first kindergarten class. Her adjustment period lasted longer than most children. Each morning, Felicia would sit sobbing and refuse to go to school. She would complain of stomachaches or headaches, or throw tantrums, anything to stay home. After a while, she settled down and did quite well throughout her school years. Eventually, Felicia discovered that she had an ability to care for people one on one, which prompted her to choose nursing as a profession.

Her recent promotion was the culmination of a great deal of work and something Felicia had yearned for, but she became extremely anxious when her boss discussed her new responsibilities. Her anxiety became overwhelming when she discovered that she had been scheduled to teach her first seminar in six weeks. Felicia panicked as she thought of all sorts of calamities that might occur while she was teaching. She was afraid that she would be at a loss for words. She was also afraid that something terrible would happen. She did not know what it would be, but she was sure that something would cause her tremendous embarrassment and humiliation. Felicia worried constantly about having to speak in public. She agonized over the next six weeks, but did her best to prepare the first lesson. Although nursing was Felicia's forté, she suddenly began to feel as if she didn't know the subject at all.

She shared her anxiety with some of the members of her women's group. They all supported her by saying that they understood how intimidating it was to speak in front of large groups, and they all promised to pray for her. Although Felicia drew comfort from their support, she couldn't overcome the feeling of impending disaster.

Felicia recalled that when she trained to become a nurse, she was asked to present a case in front of her peers. She remembered how anxious and worried she felt. In fact, the mere thought of it, seemed to make the room spin around her. She recalled the beads of sweat that developed on her brow and her heart pounding like a drum as she stood before her peers. Felicia still found it hard to believe that she was able to get through that presentation so many years ago. She recalled that after it was all over, she promised herself she would never be in a public speaking situation ever again.

How could this happen? How could she, who was so comfortable in a social setting at work, at home, and in her church, be in such turmoil about speaking before a group of her peers? When she thought about the big picture and what this promotion meant to her, she realized that she was looking at things in a distorted way. How could teaching seminars cause such upset in her life? But she had to admit to herself that it did.

Felicia was now more irritable and distracted when she was with her family. She did not feel the comfort and ease that she normally felt. Her mind was preoccupied with the thoughts of having to teach. She readily admitted her fears to her husband who did his best to reassure her.

Felicia noticed that her fears about public speaking began to affect her attendance at church. Previously she was comfortable in shar-

Imagined fears of humiliation under the scrutiny of others when required to do public speaking or performing results in the physical and psychological feelings of anxiety.

ing thoughts, ideas, and information at her church meetings. But because of the fears surrounding her new job, she found that she was now also afraid of speaking at church meetings. She had a vague aching notion that she would humiliate herself. When she questioned herself as to what she thought might happen, she could not figure it out. Would she stutter in front of everyone and look like a fool? Would she turn beet-red and call attention to herself? Would she be so frightened that she would pass out in front of everybody?

Sometimes during the meetings she felt as if her whole body was tense. Her distress was noticeable to her friends and many members of her church. One day, her pastor approached her and asked if he could speak to her. With a sigh of relief, she walked into his office and began to pour out all the fears that had been troubling her. She indicated that her new job required public speaking—something she was intensely afraid of—and that this fear was beginning to affect other areas in her life. The pastor thought for a moment, and then he stated, "I think I know what you're going through. In fact, earlier in my life, I had to deal with a similar problem. When I was training in the seminary, I discovered that I was fearful of speaking in public settings. It caused me a great deal of pain to think that I was called to be a minister but that I could not feel comfortable preaching from the pulpit. Fortunately, there was help. When I relayed my problems to my professor, he offered to work with me personally in overcoming my phobia. If that didn't help, he said he would recommend someone with professional expertise to address my fear. Although I was very close to dropping out of the seminary, I took him up on his offer. As you can see, it worked."

Discussion

One of the kindest interventions one person can offer to another is an acknowledgement of that person's suffering. When Felicia's pastor empathized with her fears and then proceeded to share his own experience, he accomplished at least two important tasks of a minister. First, he comforted Felicia in letting her know that fear, albeit distorted, can be a normal human emotion and that even "men of God," like himself, can be subject to it. Secondly, his testimony of his own road to mastery, aided by counseling, provided hope and a solution to Felicia's problem. Testimonies represent a powerful means of support from one Christian to another. In the area of mental health, there are benefits when Christians who have recovered from a psychiatric condition share their experience with another sufferer. The message that professional help is available and that emotional difficulties do not mean weak faith or character flaw is conveyed. This kind of sharing from one

Christian to another represents a powerful supportive intervention and plays an important role in the strength of the church community.

Felicia's story demonstrates all the symptoms of a common condition known as "social phobia," also called "social anxiety disorder." Imagined fears of humiliation under the scrutiny of others when required to do public speaking or performing results in the physical and psychological feelings of anxiety. Intense fear and preoccupation with the feared situation occurs. Also problematic are the physical symptoms of anxiety such as palpitations, shaking, stomach upset, dry mouth, and sweating.

Many of us can appreciate that it is normal for one to have a certain amount of anxiety when a new challenge is presented. On the surface, Felicia's plight does not seem quite so serious. However, if the fear causes prolonged distress (typically over six months) and interferes with everyday function, the condition should be evaluated in order to take the next step.

First, one should obtain every opportunity to rehearse or practice the feared activity. In Felicia's case, speaking in front of people is the feared situation. She should progress via gradual steps to reach the goal of public speaking, even if it causes some distress in the beginning. Perhaps she could begin by visiting the lecture rooms. Practicing her lessons alone or with a few trusted friends may be a good start. She could then spend time with the students in smaller groups and graduate to larger ones. Whatever the case, she should not avoid the feared situation. This will only prolong the mastery of her fears. If this does not afford sufficient progress, she should obtain advice from an expert in social phobia or anxiety disorders. Many university medical centers have stress and anxiety programs. These programs offer staff therapists, physicians, and researchers who can do an appropriate evaluation.

Psychological treatments include programs of gradual exposure to the feared situation. The process by which the patient gets used to the situation is called desensitization. The patient is gradually taught, through repeated practice and homework assignments, the various techniques and processes required to learn to control the fear. Therapy can be done on an individual or group basis depending on the needs of the patient. Medications are sometimes indicated and can prove to be helpful. They are often used just prior to the time of performance and can quell anxiety, palpitations, and the other manifestations of social phobia.

> If you are going to overcome the fear of speaking or performing in public, you may need to "wage war" on this anxiety in a variety of ways until it is defeated.

Drugs known as beta-blockers can slow down heart rate and block palpitations. Other medications such as benzodiazepines can be used just prior to public speaking to calm the emotional aspects of anxiety. Examples include alprazolam (Xanax) or clonazepam (Klonopin). These medications should be used carefully as they may cause sedation. Prolonged use may cause drug dependence, and simultaneous alcohol use must be avoided. However if used properly, under the guidance of a physician, medications can be very helpful to the sufferer.

The very fear of exposing oneself to the distress one experiences from anxiety in social situations makes it hard to seek assistance from others. In general, people with social phobia have to overcome this hurdle before obtaining treatment. Many fail to do so. Acknowledging a problem and seeking appropriate advice paves the road for the Christian to gain mastery. In the Old Testament, the author of Proverbs counsels, "Listen to advice and accept discipline, and at the end you will be counted among the wise," (19:20), and, "Plans are established by seeking advice; so if you wage war, obtain guidance" (20:18).

In a sense, Felicia's preparation for her new job is a metaphoric "waging of war." She has to battle her fear, and she recognizes that it has been a lifelong struggle. Under the conditions of this new job, she realizes that her fear will jeopardize her ability to perform if she does not get help. After listening to the pastor's advice, she may choose to seek help or she may ignore his suggestions. If she indeed does have social phobia, in other words, this problem persists to the point where she is not able to carry out her responsibilities, then the wisest approach is to obtain professional help.

Supportive advice from one's own experience as a Christian may begin to help others find answers to their problems. Felicia's pastor did this very well. However, there are subtle barriers to providing empathic advice. A major but subtle obstacle is the stigma of having a psychological problem, which renders the sufferer unwilling to complain, and those who have gone through the experience unwilling to share. It took courage for the pastor to reveal that he had a problem that required psychological help. He had to overcome his own sense of imperfection and the stigma of how he might be viewed by his peers.

I once presented this character, "Felicia," at a Christian conference. The audience reacted vehemently to her diagnosis of "social phobia," stating, "There's nothing wrong with her. She's absolutely normal." I replied, "That's exactly right. She is normal." What did they mean by the word "normal?" Does it mean that Felicia is "normal" because if they were in the same position, they would feel just as anxious? In other words, rather than saying she is "normal," they meant to say she is only being "human." Did they mean that her reaction is not uncommon and would be expected to happen to many others in the same circumstance? Did they mean that social phobia is a statistically common condition?

Some college students taking a course in "abnormal psychology" begin to view all psychological diagnoses as being abnormal or aberrant. They may even fear that they have the condition they are studying and thus be labeled "abnormal." A judgment value has now been placed on the word "abnormal."

It is this notion of "normality" that poses confusion in the attempt to treat social phobia. While normalizing anxiety in Felicia's case can be a supportive approach, it should not be used as the excuse to dismiss her complaints and ignore treatment options. Felicia is "normal." She is a normal person, but she has a condition that causes her tremendous distress, which would benefit from treatment. In fact, all of the people I have written about in this book are normal. Just because they have an anxiety disorder does not mean they are "abnormal."

In most people's minds, the stigma of a mental condition causes them to equate the illness with the person, rendering them somehow "abnormal." There are many struggling with anxiety or other disorders serving in our churches and most of them would be grateful if others did not define or judge them by their illness. After all, how would you like to be described to a newcomer as, "This is Betty. She has a mental condition, but we're praying for her."

As for the other definitions of the word "normal," social phobia is a statistically common disorder and, like many psychological conditions, is often missed and therefore untreated. The statement, "Anxiety is normal," meaning that it is "human" and therefore normal, is correct only in the following sense. Anxiety is a normal human emotion and is at times needed to help sharpen us for new challenges or alert us to danger. However, the crippling forms of anxiety that ultimately prevent people from functioning or accomplishing their goals cannot be merely accepted as normal and human. Furthermore, we cannot maintain the belief that since this is "normal," there is no need for treatment. If Felicia were to adopt this line of thinking, she might not be adequately prepared for the promotion and might become overwhelmed, anxiety-ridden, and demoralized. If she could no longer work, the question whether her anxiety is normal or not normal would be moot. The important question is, "Can she be helped?" The answer is "Yes."

How People Can Help

1. Facilitate practice sessions or rehearsals for the person with performance anxiety. For example, if Felicia thought she would feel fairly comfortable in giving her lecture to one or two people, provide her with an opportunity to do so. Or she may start with speaking a few minutes at a time, rather than giving an entire lecture. The next step might be increasing the number in the audience or prolonging the time spent lecturing. These practice sessions should be as frequent as time permits. They should be managed according to the person's level of comfort, keeping in mind that there should be increasing levels of difficulty with each step in order to reach the ultimate goal of public speaking at the job site.

2. Help offset the person's negative self-evaluation which contributes to the fear of humiliation. This chain of thought plagues the sufferer with social phobia. Generally, the person is anxious because he or she is afraid that his or her presentation will be awful. The presenter worries that he will do something embarrassing or that he may be humiliated by his appearance. He may be afraid of turning beet red, stuttering uncontrollably, or appearing foolish. The person suffering from social phobia tends to be his own most severe critic because he imagines himself in the worst light.

Caring friends can try to understand these imagined negative self-evaluations and challenge them. They can provide encouragement and realistic feedback to the speaker so that he or she does not maintain unreal, pessimistic interpretations. Encouragement and positive, realistic feedback are great tools to help in the practice session or in individual conversations with the sufferer. This, combined with genuine attempts to improve lecturing, will serve the sufferer well.

3. If the person does not appear to be helped by these tactics, think about suggesting professional help. Do not be critical of the sufferer as he is genuinely in more distress than most can imagine. Empathize with his or her suffering in order to prompt him or her to seek treatment. Gently help the person understand that he has options and that he should choose the most favorable one. He should not relinquish a much-desired opportunity because of his phobia.

Note how Felicia had made a decision earlier in life never to do public speaking again after her anxiety episode in school. The reason for this is that while she was up in front of the class, she developed physical symptoms of anxiety that are generated by over activation of the autonomic nervous system. This system, also known as the sympathetic and parasympathetic nervous system, is responsible for the rapid heart rate, sweating, flushing, and sensation of anxiety. When a person leaves the feared activity or situation, there is a decrease in the activity of this system resulting in what the person feels to be an "improvement." Thus, they have learned that avoidance of such activity reduces the activation of these symptoms. This leads them to completely avoid these activities.

Others may notice this, but often it is subtle and unnoticed by friends and family. Unfortunately, this avoidant behavior worsens the phobia, as the person never has the opportunity to learn to master his fears. You may be able to help by understanding how avoidance behavior is maintained. You can point out subtle avoidance practices and encourage exposure to fears. As a person is gradually exposed to the feared activity, the autonomic nervous system is activated and the person will become anxious. Eventually, however, the anxiety is reduced through a process called "habituation." In other words, a person's nervous system and thought processes adjust to handle the anxiety. This is produced by regular exposure to the feared situation.

Since the person who is suffering may not be as inclined to seek treatment as you are to help, it may fall to you to research possible sources of help for your friend. Places where one can seek help in mastering the fear of public speaking are teaching universities with accredited clinical psychology programs. Many of them operate clinics which are staffed by competent clinicians who also supervise PhD or Doctorate in Psychology students. For social phobia, look for a psychology program that has a strong "cognitive-behavioral" orientation. This tends to be the method of treatment most helpful for phobias. The American Psychological Association has a listing of accredited clinical psychology doctoral programs.

4. If you are in training at the seminary level, you can help your peers by identifying those who may be struggling with fears like these. Seminary training requires students to take on a role that involves speaking in public. For most, this is accomplished with training and minimal anxiety. For some, it is a greater obstacle, particularly for those who are prone to be shy or for those who may have some form of performance anxiety or social phobia. Because avoidant behavior is common in anxiety disorders, a person suffering from social phobia or performance anxiety will typically react by dropping out without apparent explanation. Fellow students, school advisors, professors, and counselors can help prevent this phenomenon by being alert to students' concerns and reasons for leaving.

In some seminaries, counseling courses and programs provide a forum to explore issues that cause anxiety among students as well as in the general community. These classes provide an opportunity to identify the anxious student who may have performance anxiety as well as other fears. However, this classroom setting would only benefit those students who participate. It will not help the anxious student who does not choose to attend such a class. A more generalized and formalized program to intervene with the anxious seminary student is needed at the dean or advisor level. This is best done in conjunction with the seminary's counseling program or a counseling course instructor. A formalized program attending to these matters may benefit not just the shy, phobic student but others as well.

Be careful not to dismiss a problem by calling it "normal." While normalizing a behavior is usually supportive, it should not end there. Try to help the person yourself, or recommend professional treatment. On the other hand, do not stigmatize or label a person as "abnormal" if he or she has intense anxiety. It is crucial that you maintain this delicate balance if you really want to help your anxiety-ridden peers.

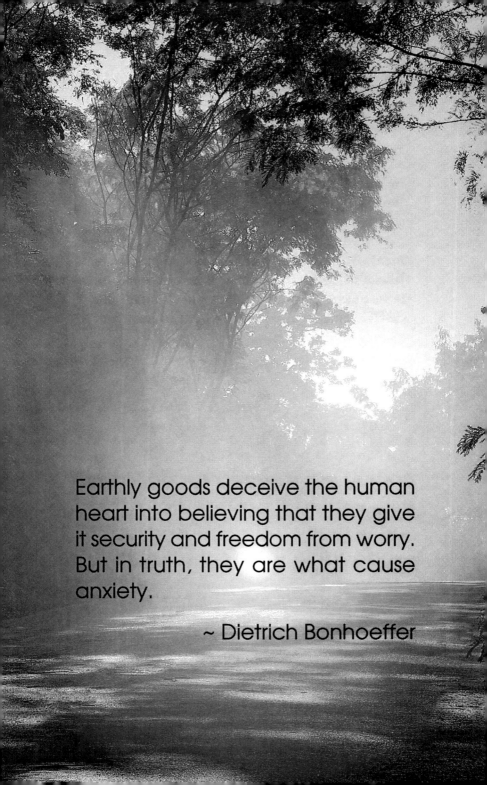

Earthly goods deceive the human heart into believing that they give it security and freedom from worry. But in truth, they are what cause anxiety.

~ Dietrich Bonhoeffer

CHAPTER 5

Generalized Anxiety
The Individual and the Church

As the teacher of the adult Sunday school, I first met Samuel two years ago. Punctual and solicitous, almost to a fault, he appeared in the Bible study classroom at least fifteen minutes early each Sunday morning. He seemed to relish the study of God's Word, and the topics he enjoyed most were church history and the doctrine of law and grace. He was an active participant, and his courteous manner enabled him to relate well to the other adult members of the class. As we all got to know each other better, we found out that Samuel, who was in his thirties, lived with his elderly parents and took care of them. He was single and worked in an office as a bookkeeper. He professed faith in the Lord and had been a Christian for many years.

One day in Bible study, we were discussing the topic of forgiveness. I noticed that Samuel had a worried look on his face. His brow was furrowed, his eyes darted back and forth, and there was a suggestion of tears welling. This was rather unusual for Samuel because he always seemed animated by these discussions and very open about his confidence in God's grace and forgiveness. He looked directly at me at the end of the session and asked whether or not worrying was a sin. Furthermore, if it were a sin, he wanted to know if constant worrying were due to "weak faith." One by one, the class members addressed their words of comfort and edification, assuring Samuel that "not all worry is sin." Someone exclaimed, "If anyone has sinned whether it be in worrying or other matters, God can forgive him if he repents." Since it was the end of the study hour, the class members left after a closing prayer. But it was clear to me that Samuel did not receive any comfort from their words. He was still deeply troubled and sat motionless in his chair. He finally got up and asked if he could speak to me at some convenient time. We agreed to meet for coffee later that afternoon.

At the local diner, Samuel poured out his story to me. Between sobs, he told me that he was worried about his parents' aging and frail health. Although there was nothing particularly new about their condition, he feared that they were not going to be there for him for long. Samuel was in fact managing his parents' affairs but felt he couldn't live without his parents' moral support. If they were to die, he feared he would be unable to function. He imagined that he would lose his job and be unable to care for himself. These worries had not always been such a problem but had become more prominent in the last six months. Smiling a little bit to himself, he said, "Well, I confess that I have always been a worrywart, but I never used to let my worries get to the point where they really affected me. I would simply pray and put these matters into God's hands." Now, however, he was concerned that all his worrying was a reflection of a weak faith. When I indicated that I didn't think so, he seemed momentarily relieved and thanked me for listening to his troubles.

Over the next couple of months, I was on the telephone with Samuel several times a week. He often called lamenting that he was worried about his parents' health and his future. I began to realize that he derived temporary comfort from each call but then resumed his worrying. I could not pinpoint anything that led to his worries, and his persistent phone calls and serious ruminations about his future began to annoy me. At times, I became frustrated and exasperated. I felt helpless and unable to do anything for him, and yet he called on me constantly to address his worries. My teaching at the Bible study class became increasingly uncomfortable. I felt trapped by his persistent questioning of God's ability to forgive and to love. His worried, pessimistic state also put a damper on the rest of the class. Gradually attendance dwindled as Samuel began to monopolize the classroom situation. I didn't know how to handle this, so I approached the pastor and the board members for their assistance. Some of them felt that Samuel might be helped if he were actively distracted in doing other things. They tried to develop some responsibilities at church that would keep him busy.

Samuel reluctantly agreed to try out the board's suggestions, and was occupied and content assisting the church secretary with some of her duties. His visits to the church office twice a week seemed to fill his time, and he developed a rapport with the secretary. However, gradually as he began to talk to her, he felt comfortable enough to share some of his problems with her. And not

If you are going to help a self-confessed "worry-wart," you should prepare to walk a fine line between supporting the person and enabling his or her litany of concerns.

surprisingly, the church secretary began to feel bombarded by his persistent worries. After some time, she felt that his presence was impeding her ability to do her work. Although she wanted to be polite, Samuel's volunteer work at the church was beginning to frustrate her as well. She also approached the pastor for help, and once again, he convened with the church board to discuss the situation.

The board wondered how Samuel, who had been a member of their church for such a long time, could have become such a problem. They asked each other whether anyone knew about anything in Samuel's life that could be upsetting him so, but nobody had an answer. Some members felt sympathy and compassion for Samuel and stated that this was a matter of being patient. Others who were more in direct contact with him guiltily expressed their feelings of frustration and helplessness. Still others were quite open in expressing their anger and felt that something should be done quickly. The pastor stated that this was a complicated situation, and he asked if a visit to Samuel's parents might not be a good idea. Not knowing what else to do, the board members agreed that it was worth a try. The pastor made plans to visit Samuel's parents, but admonished the board, "If the feelings that are being generated in this church continue, I fear that Samuel will not stay in our midst for long. It would not take long for Samuel to sense the frustration of his peers and leave our church. I want you all to understand this because I've seen it happen again and again."

Discussion

> So that there should be no division in the body, but that its parts should have equal concern for each other. If one part suffers, every part suffers with it; if one part is honored, every part rejoices with it. Now you are the body of Christ, and each one of you is a part of it (1 Corinthians 12:25-27).

When mental illness occurs in the church, everyone is affected. Scripture supports this and tells us that as a body, we not only rejoice together but at times we suffer together especially when one member is hurting. A difficult and challenging problem confronting many pastors and lay leaders is what to do when one member is afflicted with psychological problems which then negatively affects other members. Hopefully, education and increased awareness of the disorder would develop sensitivity and insight into the problem. This, combined with the biblical exhortation to work as a body may make the church one of the best support networks for people afflicted with anxiety.

Samuel is suffering from generalized anxiety disorder. His problem is identified by the fact that he has been suffering from excessive worry for the past six months. These worries center around his aging parents as well as his ability to sustain his job should they die. Although there is no evidence for the immediacy of his fears, he finds that his worries are excessive and difficult, if not impossible to control. Interestingly, he alludes to this, showing some insight, when he labels himself as always being a "worry-wart." However, even he has noticed that in the past six months his worries are getting out of hand.

Often, people with generalized anxiety disorder find that they are unable to control their worries and that these worries become pervasive and eventually affect their ability to function socially or occupationally. Certainly, if it doesn't affect their ability to function, generalized anxiety disorder may cause severe distress. This disorder is also characterized by associated symptoms such as restlessness or feeling keyed up, easy fatigability, difficulty in concentration, muscle tension, or some form of sleep disturbance.[1]

If you were to ask Samuel about any of these features in the past six months, he would be likely to report that on most days, he experiences shakiness, tension in his muscles, and feels tired. He might also report that sometimes at work his "mind has gone blank," which then contributes to his worries that he may lose his job. This, then, becomes a vicious cycle as he begins to dwell on a series of catastrophic thoughts, such as his parents' dying, poverty after losing his job, and the inability to support himself.

Sufferers from this disorder pose a dilemma in the church setting. Many times the excessive worry of such people develops a life of its own and has significant effects on church activities, such as the monopolization of Bible studies or of people's time with the repeated expression of excessive worries and the demands for reassurance. This may be a source of frustration and anger for the church members. Many people who do not suffer from this problem find it difficult to understand or even tolerate the excessive worries of their fellow church member. They attempt to reassure the person with biblical truths but are exasperated when this yields only temporary results and the patient reverts to his worrisome thinking. It is important to understand that such people find it difficult to control their worries and that this is a hallmark of the disorder. It is not only an individual problem but begins to be a problem for the entire church body.

After several board meetings in Samuel's church, the pastor recognized that the negative reactions Samuel's problem was generating among his peers could lead to potential ostracism. Therefore, recognition and a better understanding of this problem is mandatory for the health of the individual as well as the life of the church. One can see that Samuel's church has made numerous thoughtful attempts to help Samuel. It is these kinds of interventions that contribute to the welfare and the support that is provided by a church when a person experiences a crisis in his life. Such interventions may help sustain such a person until he is able to overcome the symptoms of generalized anxiety disorder.

It takes the wisdom of Solomon combined with the patience of Job for a fellowship of believers to have a "Samuel" in their midst week after week without reservation or resentment.

However, there may be a tipping point for some individuals where professional help is warranted.

Psychological treatments and medications for generalized anxiety disorder exist. It is quite clear that numerous individuals have benefited from therapy. Additionally, individuals may also benefit from psychiatric and medical evaluation as there are many other illnesses which can occur in the presence of generalized anxiety disorder or mimic its features. Once recognized, these other disorders can then be treated. Such disorders would include clinical depression, adjustment disorders, substance/medication-induced anxiety disorder, or anxiety disorder due to another medical condition. All these problems are amenable to treatment and the benefits of improved functioning are valuable.

How People Can Help

By way of "prescriptive" information for the church leader, we can extract important lessons from Samuel's case.

1. Caring people made the effort to listen to Samuel's story, sharing in the burden and then praying for him. No doubt, caring people made multiple attempts to comfort him. Proverbial wisdom teaches us that kind words are capable of cheering a man whose heart is weighed by anxiety. Although the effect may be temporary, it still helps.

2. The church members involved with Samuel were honest with their own feelings of frustration, which facilitated discussion with their pastor about the possible ramifications of these resentments. They convened as often as needed in a group employing problem-solving approaches and prayer.

Hopefully, one of the issues they addressed was how to minister to Samuel without sacrificing the viability of the Sunday school class or the functions of the church secretary. They offered Samuel a place to work, which occupied his spare time.

3. Caring people made efforts to do more fact finding in order to help Samuel. The pastor offered to visit the parents.

4. Caring people continued to listen, even when it felt like nothing was changing. They continued to provide a "listening ear," believing that the process alone would be experienced as supportive, even if no solutions were offered. No one was looking for a quick fix; in cases of generalized anxiety disorder, there is rarely a quick solution.

5. Caring people acknowledged their own limitations and the roles they could play. They did not try to become heroes able to solve Samuel's problem. Instead, they directed him to appropriate sources of professional help, while remaining with him as he made use of it.

One minister reported that when a particular member experienced a change in mood, he would ask if the person had had a recent medical check-up. Sometimes, a person supposedly suffering from generalized anxiety disorder has another condition that manifests itself initially with mood changes. A checkup would reveal whether or not this is the case. Caring people, when they realize professional help is warranted, make the referral even at the risk of offending the individual or being spurned. In Samuel's case professional psychological help would be beneficial. Appropriate treatment along with the support of his church should pave the road for a good outcome.

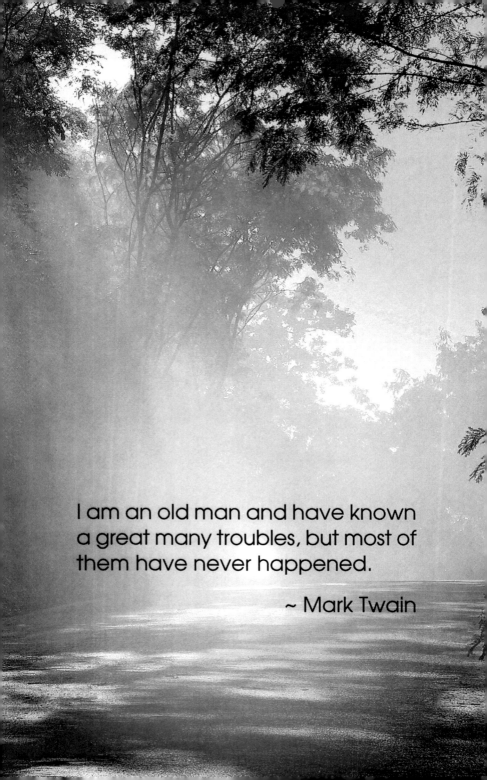

CHAPTER 6

Phobias

D R. CHARLES CONNOLLY WAS A SUCCESSFUL OPHTHALMOLO-gist of Afro American descent. He was raised in a Christian home and always felt that he was called to go to the mission field. After finishing medical school and graduating with honors, he entered into specialty training in ophthalmology. He was a skilled physician and quickly earned the respect of his colleagues. When he graduated, he established a successful practice. He received an appointment at a university hospital where he was engaged in teaching medical students as well as doing research.

Charles had never forgotten his dream of serving as a medical missionary, but because of the demands of his ophthalmology practice and his involvement in the university hospital, he felt that he had to delay his aspirations of serving the Lord abroad. He envisioned that at some point in his career he would need to make a major life decision in order to enter the mission field.

Life went very smoothly for Charles, and he was very active in a local Christian church. Soon, he met a lovely woman whom he married. After several years, he had become the father of two children, and in many respects, his life was quite fulfilled. Maintaining an active interest in the missions committee of his church, he often investigated and reported on various missionary activities to the church members and invited their support. He shared his dreams of the mission field with his family, and his wife was extremely supportive.

One year, Charles was attending a regional retreat where he learned of a specialized medical organization that went abroad to various countries to assist in addressing the extensive health needs of the underserved. This organization's ships transported doctors, nurses, medical supplies, and operating room facilities to various ports internationally and would provide professional care for the indigent population on board. Intrigued by this particular mission program, Charles requested more information. He was delighted and surprised to hear that they were looking for an ophthalmologist to serve among the population in Africa where there was an alarming high rate of eye diseases. In fact, they were desperately looking for an ophthalmologic surgeon to address these needs. Would Dr. Connolly be available at any time? This was the chance of a lifetime.

Charles recognized that he finally had to make the difficult decision. He would have to leave his practice and the comfort of his professional community to fulfill his dream. Yes, there was a lot of personal sacrifice to be made. On the other hand, this was the challenge that he had always desired. Since he was a young boy, Charles had prayed that the Lord would send him to the mission field. After much prayer and discussion with his wife and members of his church, Charles applied to this mission organization. Two weeks later he received an acceptance letter. He and his family would be sent abroad within three months' time. Things were moving very quickly for Charles and his family. They carefully planned all the details of their move and began saying goodbye to their friends and family. Things seemed to be going quite smoothly for the family. Although their schedules were very busy, they looked forward with anticipation to their new environment. There were going to be new schools, responsibilities, a new home, and many challenges to meet.

During this time of preparation Charles awoke one day from a frightening dream. In it, he was attacked by a large coiling snake. He awoke from his nightmare soaked in perspiration and began to recall his childhood fear of snakes. He had almost forgotten about this phobia, and in fact, it had receded into the back of his mind. After all how many snakes does one become exposed to in a large city? Now his fear reappeared. Realizing that he would most likely be sent to places where snakes were endemic to the area, he became frantic. *How utterly ridiculous,* he rationalized, *that a simple fear like this could actually rob me of the joy of my plans to go abroad!* But the more he thought, the more fearful he became. In fact, now the anticipation of this medical mission project was overshadowed by consternation and worry. The thought of snakes and the fear of being bitten by them became Charles' major preoccupation. His wife noticed that his preparations for the trip began to lose their fervor and excitement. In fact, her husband seemed reluctant to talk about the trip. This was rather perturbing for her; therefore, she decided to confront him.

Phobias cause intense anxiety characterized by physical symptoms such as sweating, palpitations, muscle tension, and gastric symptoms.

Discussion

Dr. Charles Connolly is suffering from a classic case of a specific phobia,[1] in this case the fear of snakes. Many people suffer from different forms of phobias—the sight of blood, injury, injections, medical tests, or a fear of animals, objects, natural environmental conditions, or certain situations. The latter can include the fear of driving or the fear of flying. Phobias cause intense anxiety characterized by physical symptoms such as sweating, palpitations, muscle tension, and gastric symptoms. Some may experience dizziness and fainting, especially those who are afraid of blood, injection, or injury. Even though it is problematic for them, adults do recognize that their fears are exaggerated. Children, on the other hand, often see their fears as being realistic and posing a real danger. Many people suffer from unrealistic fears. They are usually not a problem unless they interfere with functioning, such as performance at work, interaction in social situations, or their general quality of life. Phobias are intense fears that last typically six months or more.

In Charles' case, his fear of snakes was not a problem until the call to the mission field. It then became the stumbling block for his ability to participate in the mission program comfortably, if at all. At this point in his life, his fears may represent a diagnosable phobia, particularly if it persists.

Psychological treatments are available for phobias. Often these include a desensitization program targeted at the feared trigger whether it be situations, objects, or other stimuli. These treatments can assist the phobic patient in coping with the feared stimulus and give him gradual tolerance of the situation or item feared. It teaches him not to avoid his fear, but to expose himself to it in a gradual way in order to master it. Without treatment, most people tend to handle their phobias by avoidance. In some cases, people endure the feared stimulus and are extremely distressed at having to do so. Avoidance can be detrimental to a person's life and most certainly hinders treatment. Unable to pursue interests that he or she would ordinarily pursue, the phobic person leads a very restricted lifestyle.

Paul's experience as recorded in Scripture offers encouragement. "For when we came into Macedonia, we had no rest, but we were harassed at every turn—conflicts on the outside, fears within. But God, who comforts the downcast, comforted us by the coming of Titus" (2 Cor. 7:5). Notice that Paul did not refrain from his work despite the "fears" and the "conflicts" and being "harassed." Observe that God provides comfort, in this case in the person of Titus. Perseverance, bolstered by confidence in God's comfort will combat the tendency toward avoidance. Perseverance is a prerequisite for a good response to psychological treatments in which a patient practices exposure to his fears in order to gain mastery.

For many Christians, mastering a phobia begins by acknowledging the fear to themselves and to God, sometimes by quoting Scriptures like Philippians 4:6-7: "Do not be anxious about anything, but in every situation, by prayer and petition, with thanksgiving, present your requests to God. And the peace of God, which transcends all understanding, will guard your hearts and your minds in Christ Jesus."

The goal of treatment in relation to phobias of people of faith is to enable them to overcome fear in order to pursue the ministries to which God has called them.

How People Can Help

1. Given that psychological treatments such as gradual desensitization works for specific phobias, it would be extremely beneficial for the church or its mission board to facilitate treatment as part of a missionary's preparation. This may take the form

of obtaining an appropriate counselor who may be part of a network of trained therapists that specialize in working with church or missionary organizations. Financial support for the treatment is one tangible way the church can show its support and to ease the financial burden of a missionary who is willing to sacrifice his current source of income to serve abroad. In paying for the treatment, the church or mission board affirms that this psychological treatment is part of the training program for missions and that the church is helping to equip the missionary for service. All missionary candidates are encouraged to participate; therefore, the process of getting mental professional help is destigmatized.

Behavioral/desensitization treatment for specific phobias is relatively short-term. This is of practical importance as Charles Connolly has three months before he travels abroad. This is a realistic time frame for this type of therapy. During this period, the mission board could optimize results by collaborating with the therapist, each playing a unique but interdependent role in helping the patient, while keeping the details of any such endeavors confidential. The psychological treatment is intended to handle the phobia in an effort to get the patient to go abroad with some level of comfort. In meeting this goal, the therapist addresses the patient's phobic avoidance, which might otherwise deter his plans.

Apart from specific phobias, there are many other issues that do arise when one is preparing for the mission field. These factors can be logistical, psychosocial, and spiritual. These issues can be handled more effectively by the mission board or the church. Hence, collaboration between the mission board and the therapist would define how each component can contribute to assist the person in preparation for the mission field.

2. In the case of Dr. Connolly, two other questions need to be addressed. Does Charles have concerns about his ability to perform in his new environment? For example, does his dream reflect anxious concerns about how he will do, especially in light of the huge transitions that he and his family will be experiencing? The second question is: Does Charles have concerns or beliefs in the role of spiritual oppression and its effect on his endeavor?

These questions are often best handled by those who have experience in preparing missionaries. There are so many issues that may be troubling Charles that need articulating. It certainly would be valuable for him to have a confidant in the church, someone with whom he feels comfortable in sharing his misgivings and anxiety. It would help him to identify for himself those areas where he feels inadequate and provide an opportunity for a caring Christian to give him a listening ear, prayer support, and guidance. The spiritual confidant should be someone of Charles's own choosing. Preferably, he or she should also be capable of understanding the issues related to mission work and the adjustments that are required. This person can be seen as a partner in the venture, helping to understand all the variables involved in order to seek the success of the mission. Didactic training provided by the sponsoring missionary organization in the form of language preparation classes, cross-cultural training, and workshops designed to impart important facts are invaluable. These can be tailored to address a missionary's particular needs and concerns.

The second question raised by this case illustration has to do with Charles' fears of spiritual oppression. The definition of this entity can be ambiguous. However, it generally refers to opposition by spiritually evil forces against the work of a Christian. It is beyond the scope of this book to define the meaning and nuances of this matter. Suffice it to say that spiritual oppression is thought to play a thwarting, discouraging role among many Christians who are about to embark on difficult but potentially life-changing ministries. Therefore, the mission board must answer the question as to whether the potential missionary is equipped with the strengths, talents, and personality profile needed to sustain the obstacles.

Although this has been a lifelong vision for Charles, it is not clear that the mission field represents the optimal setting for the effective use of his talents, training, and experience. In order to find out, he might be wise to first participate in a short-term medical mission effort. Where possible, he should not completely sever his current professional responsibilities, but maintain a clear opportunity to return. For example, taking a sabbatical from work to explore missions is one way to see if one can be a full-time missionary without cutting off established options. Short-term missions may provide the best means of keeping one's options open, and thus reduce the anxiety that can accompany major life changes. At some point in the future, when adjustments have been made and experience is gained, the person can make a better informed full-time commitment to the mission field.

3. Encourage the wife and family as part of the missionary team. Until now, we have been looking at Charles' psychological, spiritual, and career issues. But it is also of vital importance to examine the issues and concerns of the wife and the family to see if there is anything that has not been addressed. While Charles' phobia may have the center stage, the family members may have a host of unverbalized concerns which must be addressed. The church and mission board needs to be attentive to family issues and equally strong support should be provided. Viewing the family as a "mission team" is an affirming stance. After all, the family may be the only constant in a setting where there are many new changes to face. Therefore, family members can learn to provide support for each other in relation to the possible obstacles each person may face, as well as challenges they may face together.

Worrying is like running on a tread-
mill . . . it gives us an opportunity to
sweat but gets us absolutely
nowhere.

~ Jason Versey

CHAPTER 7

Agoraphobia

*Y*OU MAY REMEMBER NANCY AND HER TREATMENT FOR PANIC disorder described in a previous chapter. Over the course of two months, she improved greatly by using her new coping skills learned in therapy. She quickly identified her unrealistic thoughts, correcting them easily to the point where it became automatic to do so. Thought stopping techniques were also useful in preventing dwelling on catastrophic misbeliefs. Other copings skills of progressive muscle relaxation accompanied by visual imagery added to her ability to stop the panic attacks before they could take hold. Nancy came to enjoy a sense of self-efficacy, which allowed her to stop panic attacks.

Nancy now wanted to face some of the situations she had avoided since her condition began. She wanted to return to fun activities with the children including going to the movies, which she had not done since her first panic attack. Driving beyond a certain distance and especially on highways limited her life, so she set that as a goal. Perhaps she could even overcome her fear of flying on an airplane so she could travel, which she had not done since her honeymoon. She hoped to do this without anxiety and embarrassment. It took some time for Nancy to want to expose herself to places restricted from her activities, but her progress in treatment gave her courage when her therapist asked if she was ready to address a condition known as agoraphobia.

Discussion

When a person begins to avoid situations that might trigger a panic attack or avoid places where he cannot flee should a panic attack occur, he has developed an anxiety disorder known as agoraphobia. The *Diagnostic and Statistical Manual of Mental Health Disorders, 5th Edition* (DSM-5) requires these patients to have two situations in which they fear not being able to escape if they were to need help, be embarrassed, or have a panic attack. The situations include fear of public transportation (planes, buses, trains, and so forth), open spaces (fields, market places, closed spaces, theaters, buildings, and so forth), crowds or lines, or being alone outside the home.[1]

These triggers consistently produce intense fear, which leads to avoidance behavior, job compromise, or social activity. Agoraphobia may vary in severity. Some people persevere and try to function despite severe discomfort, but the majority of patients with this disorder are avoidant, and if untreated, the avoidance becomes chronic. They can become virtually housebound and rely on others to meet their needs. Early intervention and treatment of this condition is crucial. It affects adolescents and young adults and may last through the life cycle. Elderly patients can be diagnosed with this condition. Their primary concerns may be that they may have a fall or that something physically humiliating such as incontinence or vomiting will occur if they leave the house. In order to appropriately assist them, it is important to evaluate whether this fear is excessive or realistic in light of their overall health.

The avoidance behavior known as agoraphobia commonly complicates the life of the individual suffering from panic attacks. In an attempt to avoid triggering anxiety, he or she avoids places where panic attacks have occurred or where there is no easy means of escape without being noticed or possibly embarrassed. How can others help such a sufferer? It is very important that the caring individual does not worsen the situation by enabling the avoidant behavior. Avoidance can lead to a restricted lifestyle with the most tragic situation of being housebound and not functional. Caring individuals may unwittingly participate in such a process and thus enable the agoraphobic to lead an increasingly restricted lifestyle. Misguided by strong feelings of sympathy for the sufferer, caring individuals can inadvertently make it easier for the individual to restrict his activities and thus "enable" him to avoid.

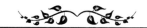

There is a balance between being too sympathetic, thus enabling avoidance, and expecting the sufferer to surmount their fears faster than they are able.

The goal of treatment is the exact opposite. Through a process of talk therapy and homework, the patient is asked to increase his exposure to the outside and especially to feared places. Hence, a caring individual must be aware of his own contribution to this process whether it be by enabling regressive, avoidant behavior which may feel more comfortable to the patient or whether it is the more positive role of encouraging the patient to move forward even though it is anxiety provoking.

For example, suppose a person is afraid to return to work because he had his first panic attack while on the train going to work. He wants to avoid traveling on the train because he believes that he will have another panic attack while riding on the train. An "enabler" would agree with the person's presumption and would support the notion that he should not go to work in order to avoid panic attacks. This is counterproductive and fosters agoraphobia. On the other hand, the caring individual would do well to coax the person to make attempts to get back on the train or simply reinforce the idea that getting back on the train is an important goal. Naturally, this is more easily said than done since excessive fear can cause a great deal of anticipatory anxiety in the person contemplating getting back on the train. When there is resistance or a great deal of difficulty, professional help can provide the means and coping skills to achieve this goal.

Caring individuals have to negotiate a balance between not being too sympathetic and thus enabling avoidance versus being too harsh and critical in expecting the sufferer to surmount their fears quickly. This process requires time and possible professional help. Perhaps the best conceptualization for the role of the caring individual, whether it is the minister or the family or a friend, is that of a good "coach." The coach congratulates the individual when he is willing to venture out and make progress despite significant anxiety but does not demoralize or criticize when a person succumbs to his fears. Such a stance would be most supportive to the sufferer. This is especially important while he or she is in treatment as it can augment the work done in therapy.

Let's turn our attention to Nancy.

Treatment

Nancy comes into her therapy session excited about the new relaxation tapes she recently purchased. She tells you that the calming nature sounds, bird songs, ocean waves, and soothing reading of Bible promises really helped her. She now has quite a collection of CDs and DVDs to use. The therapist takes notes while Nancy suggests items she would like to work on to increase her exposure to situations which she has avoided. Together they create a hierarchy ranging from what Nancy tells her is the least anxiety-provoking to the most, going from one to ten. The therapist completes the list, makes a copy for Nancy and tells her that they will be working on this exposure hierarchy for the next series of sessions until Nancy reaches her goals. The hierarchy looks like the following:

1. Walking to the theater and purchasing a movie ticket for a future showing.
2. Going out to eat in a restaurant.
3. Discussing with my children about the movie we will see.
4. Drive to the highway.
5. Driving to the next town with my friend.
6. Driving alone to the next town.
7. Going to the movie theater where I had a panic attack to watch the movie with my family.
8. Checking websites for air tickets.
9. Booking a ticket and driving to the airport numerous times.
10. Taking the flight.

Nancy works with the therapist to accomplish each goal, practicing as many times as possible during the week for homework. If the task should prove too difficult, they would divide the task into two parts in order to slow down the exposure. For example, Nancy was really afraid of returning to the movie theater. So she decided to go first with her husband to a restaurant for dinner and walk to the theater to get on line as if she were going in. They would then repeat this during the weekend and try to see the movie with the reassurance that she could leave after thirty minutes if she wanted. This is a negotiating type of experience with the therapist and Nancy learns that she can create modifications for useful homework practices. Before long, Nancy sees that she is making progress, which motivates her to advance through the hierarchy. The treatment reaches a climax when Nancy is able to take a vacation at Disney World with her family!

How People Can Help

1. Assist sufferers to get help early.

2. Do not foster avoidant behavior or enable a person to lead an avoidant lifestyle.

3. Be gentle in helping the person increasingly expose themselves to feared situations.

4. Collaborate with them to create exposure exercises and allow them to practice each step until they feel comfortable enough to take the next step.

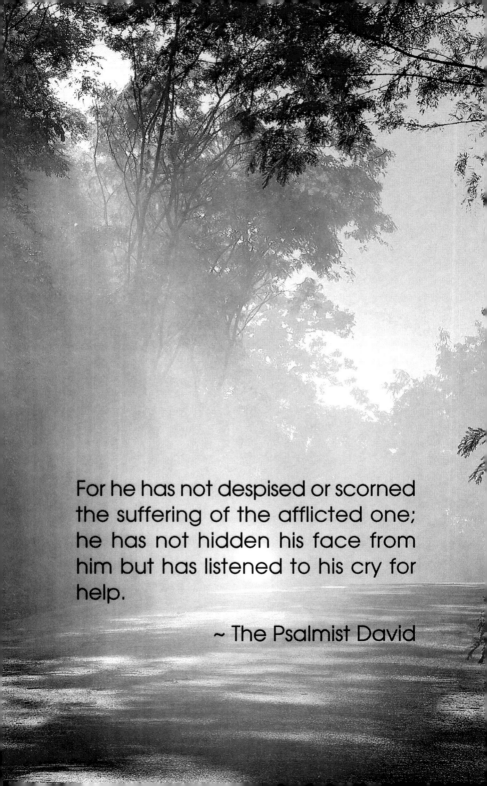

For he has not despised or scorned the suffering of the afflicted one; he has not hidden his face from him but has listened to his cry for help.

~ The Psalmist David

CHAPTER 8

Post-Traumatic Stress Disorder
A Specific Case

*G*REETING NEW PEOPLE IN THE CHURCH WAS ALWAYS A THRILL of mine. These people are potential new members, new people who could be introduced to God's love and grace or they can be "angels" in our midst. As president of the ladies guild, I often enjoyed inviting the new women to come to our church lunches, our women's meetings, or to my home for a nice dinner. One Sunday morning I spotted a new couple sitting in the back row of our church. The woman was in her twenties, thin, and had a pretty, innocent, child-like face. The man, on the other hand, was tall, robust, and had very handsome features. They were an attractive couple. I made up my mind to introduce myself to them at the end of the service. As the last hymn was being sung, I slowly made my way to the back of the church.

"Hello," I cheerfully said. "My name is Ellen. I'd like to welcome you to our church." The couple smiled and they thanked me politely for my greeting. When they made an effort to quickly leave, I intercepted and asked the woman, "Are you new in town?" She said in a small weak voice, "Yes, we just moved here and I haven't met very many people yet. We're just looking for a church to attend every Sunday." I quickly replied, "Well, you're more than welcome to attend our woman's luncheon. We have it every Tuesday at 11:00. Would you like to join us?" She looked at her husband and then turned to me and said, "I'd like to think about it. Let me get back to you." And with this she said good-bye and they left.

The following day I dropped by the church and checked the church registration book and found their names and a telephone number. I came home and gave them a call. She answered and sounded very happy to hear my voice. She stated that she would love to attend the woman's luncheon the next week and asked whether she could bring anything. I said no, and offered her a lift to the meeting.

At the luncheon she appeared bright and animated, eager to talk about all sorts of recipes and homemaking ideas. She indicated that she had grown up in a Christian home and had some Bible training as a child. She stated that this luncheon was just the thing she needed in this brand new town. Over the weeks she continued to attend the meetings and was bright and talkative and motivated to learn about the Bible. She related well to the other women in the group and quickly made many friends. It was about the fifth week when suddenly she stopped attending our meetings. In fact, she was absent for the next several meetings, so the women's group decided that someone should call her.

That Sunday, to my surprise she and her husband were not present at the

Deborah was sobbing. Her voice was shaky and she asked if I could come over. "I'm really worried and upset and I just need somebody to be with me," she said.

church as they customarily had been for the past two months. I poked my head into the pastor's office and I asked him whether or not he had seen Deborah and Quentin. He indicated that he had not seen or spoken to them. That afternoon I called her number and she answered the phone. I mentioned to her that we were all concerned about her and that we hadn't seen her for a while. She said that she was sorry that she had not been able to attend the meetings because she had not been feeling well lately and promised that she would come as soon as she could. I asked whether or not there was anything I could do for her and she replied politely, "No, thank you."

Quite by accident I bumped into Deborah at the supermarket. To my amazement she appeared startled to see me and I noticed that she wore quite a bit more make-up than I had been used to. She quickly grabbed several articles of produce, dropped them in her basket, and apologized that she was in a rush. Did I notice a faint limp as she quickly rolled her wagon towards the cashier? I felt greatly disturbed but I didn't understand why.

A couple of months went by and because of the hectic holiday season I forgot about Deborah. She had not been present at any of the women's meetings and her church attendance with her husband was sporadic. Periodically, when I did think of her I quickly dismissed the thought and told myself, "Well, she will be back when she is ready."

One day I received a phone call out of the blue. Deborah was on the phone. She was sobbing. Her voice was shaky and she asked if I could come over. I naturally said yes but I asked, "Is there anything wrong?" And she replied, "I think I need some company right now. I'm really worried and upset and I just need somebody to be with me." The two-mile drive didn't take very long, but during that time many thoughts went through my head: *What could be wrong? What was I about to face?*

When I knocked at the door it opened a small crack to reveal Deborah huddled by the wall with her hand loosely on the doorknob. She was physically shaking and had a look of fright in her eyes that I had not seen there before. Her eyes were darting from the door to the living room and back to the door at me again. She appeared like such a frightened animal or even reminded me of a prisoner of war trapped in some horrible cellar. I asked her to sit down and as I held her arm I could feel her trembling in my grasp. She told me that she didn't know what was wrong but she felt that something terrible was going to happen and that she didn't know whether she was going to be able to survive to the next week. She seemed very easily startled by the different household noises and I asked her if she wanted me to fix her something to eat. She replied no, she hadn't been able to eat in quite some time. She mentioned that her appetite and strength seemed to be all gone. As I glanced down on her leg I noticed a big bruise and I asked her, "How did you get that?" She replied, "Oh, I just fell down the steps. It's just a bad bruise, there's no bones broken."

Deborah admitted that she had been having a lot of bad dreams and that her sleep had been disturbed each night. They were all frightening, violent dreams but she couldn't remember the details. She just wanted someone to be with her to pray with her and comfort her. She felt that everything was doom and gloom, and that her future was somehow foreshortened.

The doorbell rang and Deborah jumped up with a start, again cowering by the wall. As she hesitatingly reached to open the door her husband appeared at the entrance. She hurriedly composed herself and greeted him with a kiss. He turned to me, smiled and said in a cordial manner, "What a surprise to have you drop in on us. It is very nice to see you." Deborah offered a half-hearted invitation for dinner but I declined, noticing that the hour was late. There was a vague sense of discomfort in the room and I couldn't shake the way Deborah had looked a few moments earlier. I politely said goodbye and headed for home.

My pastor called me on the telephone one day. "Ellen, I just got a call from the hospital, Deborah has been hospitalized. She has had an accident and she asked if you and I could come visit her." I quickly replied, "Yes, I'll be right there." I got dressed and made my way to the hospital where I met the pastor. We went to the orthopedic ward and we discovered Deborah in a room, her body bandaged in many areas and a cast on her leg. Her face appeared puffy and bruised and she had a vacant look on her face. As we approached the bed, she turned to us and she smiled weakly.

"Are you alright?" I asked. She apologized for troubling us and she said she was such an idiot to have been so clumsy. She was, however, very glad that we came to visit her and she seemed comforted in the fact that we were in the room although she didn't say very much to us. The nurse came into the room to give her a shot of a painkiller and as she drifted off to sleep the pastor and I decided to go out into the hallway. I turned to him abruptly in the hallway and I said, "Pastor, there is something seriously wrong with Deborah. And for a while I couldn't figure out what it was. But I think it has something to do with this accident or at least this so-called accident. I don't believe it."

Discussion

This composite case illustrates the ominous but real problem of abuse as it occurs in the church community. It often takes a perceptive individual to recognize the occurrence of abuse, as there is a whole host of factors that can disguise its presence. Deborah, who is the victim of spousal abuse, is experiencing classical symptoms of Post-Traumatic Stress Disorder or PTSD. This disorder represents predictable responses to an extreme stressor, which is beyond the scope of usual human experience. These predictable human responses have been studied well in the wartime condition seen in soldiers called "shell shock."

It is not clear why many victims remain in an abusive relationship. Victims may feel trapped and perceive that there are no other options, or feelings of shame may prevent reporting the matter. Various other factors and theories may explain different individual cases.

One of the hallmarks of this disorder is the fact that the person develops amnesia or a psychic numbing as to the event of the abuse. Although the victim is repeatedly traumatized, he or she may be unable to recall various aspects of the physical abuse. In the attempt to avoid the pain of remembering the abuse, the person will often proceed with daily life as if nothing had occurred. But because of the symptoms of PTSD, which is a response to extreme trauma, such as being exposed to threatened death or serious injury to self or loved one, repeated exposure to results of violence in the workplace such as in the case of first responders handling human remains repeatedly, or being a recipient of multiple acts of sexual or physical violence, the patient usually has a number of physical and psychological manifestations.

One such symptom includes recurrent dreams of the trauma as in the case of Deborah. A victim can suffer from intrusive thoughts and images of the trauma, and may mentally re-experience the trauma in episodes called "flashbacks." Despite attempts to avoid anything associated with the trauma, the body may react with physical symptoms of anxiety. Such symptoms would include insomnia, irritability, difficulty concentrating, guardedness, and easy startling. Others with PTSD may develop dissociative symptoms such as depersonalization or derealization. The former can be described as having "out of body" experiences, while the latter is a condition where the patient does not experience the environment as being real.[1] Domestic violence is a multifaceted problem.

The victim is in tremendous need of medical as well as psychological treatment. Protection from the abuser is mandatory and may require legal maneuvers. The person who suffers from PTSD has a real sense of a foreshortened future. Often he or she has a sense of estrangement from others. This can make it quite difficult for others who wish to assist in the matter. Often people are not quite sure how to handle these situations. It is important that one should become familiar with the various resources within a state, where one can get information as to how to deal with this crisis. Sources may include hospitals, domestic violence agencies, law enforcement, or abuse hotlines. In some states abuse telephone resources may be conducted in English, Spanish, or other languages.

The National Domestic Violence Hotline, telephone number, 1-800-799-SAFE (7233) is an important resource for situations of actual or potential domestic violence. People who call this hotline are provided a safe and confidential opportunity to discuss their fears regarding violence in their home. Abused women are often isolated. Thus, having a twenty-four-hour hotline is invaluable. The hotline is a federally and privately funded resource that serves all fifty states plus Puerto Rico and the Virgin Islands. They have an extensive database referral system that can identify crucial services in the victim's local community. This includes domestic violence agencies, counselors, housing, legal services, hospitals, and law enforcement organizations. They will even contact the local police if the victim requests it. The local police department is a ready source of help. Some operate sophisticated domestic violence programs. Shelters, particularly those for abused women and children, provide a safe haven and access to community resources.

The fact that abuse can occur in the Christian community is tragic. The fact that it may be ignored is unconscionable. The church can do a vital job of assisting its helpless members.

The American Medical Association has established certain guidelines regarding the handling of victims of domestic violence.

In addition to protection for these women, treatment is recommended whether it be in individual counseling with an experienced therapist or support groups. The Christian community may be at a disadvantage in recognizing situations of abuse. The seemingly upright character of the abuser misleads many. In such circumstances, where much is kept secret, it would not be surprising that it continues to be unrecognized. The fact that abuse can occur in the Christian community is tragic. The fact that it may be ignored is unconscionable. It would serve the church well to be educated about this issue and to assist its helpless members.

He lies in wait near the villages;
from ambush he murders the innocent.
His eyes watch in secret for his victims;
like a lion in cover he lies in wait.
He lies in wait to catch the helpless;
he catches the helpless and drags them off in his net.
His victims are crushed, they collapse;
they fall under his strength.
He says to himself, "God will never notice;
he covers his face and never sees."
Psalm 10:8-11

How People Can Help

1. Never assume that domestic violence would not occur in a Christian home. The fact of the matter is that it does occur. Ministers can play an important role in addressing the problem of domestic violence. They may be approached by their constituents in a case of suspected abuse and asked to handle the situation. Therefore it is crucial that ministers obtain training in domestic violence and

understand the different types of abuse, whether it is physical, sexual, or emotional. They should be informed about the signs and symptoms of battered women and develop a network of social, medical, and legal resources in their community. If they do not have any experience in the matter, they can obtain speakers with expertise to provide workshops in this area.

Some churches, especially in metropolitan areas, organize crisis counseling services and support groups for battered women. A minister, aware of the need for these types of services in his community, can be instrumental in instituting these programs, perhaps under the auspices of his church's women's ministries. Under these conditions, training should be provided not only to the minister but also to the counselors who will be assisting battered women.

2. Caring Christians should look for changes in personality or behavior. An extroverted, friendly woman can suddenly be withdrawn, irritable, or fearful. They may not want to be touched. They may suddenly withdraw from participation in their usual activities, making excuses such as, "I am not feeling well." Watch for marked change in clothing attire or heavy makeup, all employed to cover up injuries. Look for other behavior changes such as avoiding eye contact with people. Refer to the signs and symptoms of post-traumatic stress disorder as outlined earlier in this chapter for further clues.

Many women are secretive about ongoing abuse.

A number of factors contribute to their reluctance to confide. Guilt and shame about the abuse, particularly in the Christian environment keep many women silent. They experience the abuse as humiliating and feel personal responsibility for it. The spouse who makes threats of repercussion often enforces secrecy. It can include potential harm to the wife, abandonment, or suicide. Many women who stay in abusive situations have grown up in a dysfunctional family environment, which fosters the perpetuation of abuse as a norm. Unfortunately, some women are silent because previous attempts to confide were ignored.

Because of the secrecy involved in domestic violence, caring individuals should be ready and attentive to listen to the fears of the victim and understand that she may be vague and not easily forthcoming with all the information. She may confide in you on one opportunity and then abruptly withdraw for fear of having exposed herself. Because this ambivalence is common, it is important to remain a consistent friend. Many people, when they become aware of such a difficult situation, feel a desire to shy away from the situation. A caring individual should remain consistent and provide safe opportunities for the woman to discuss her predicament. During these talks, you can bolster her self-esteem, which has been terribly damaged. Indicate to her that she is NOT to blame for the abuse. This is a common false perception in battered women. They usually have been told by the abuser, and thus believe, that they are being beaten because of something they have done. They should be told that physical and sexual abuse is a crime perpetrated by the abuser that is punishable by law.

Strengthen the woman's Christian identity and counsel them that as women of God, they are created to have a loving and respectful relationship with their spouse and are not designed by God to be an object of abuse. When abuse does occur, it reflects a violation of God's standard as well as a criminal act. Caring individuals can provide this type of spiritual instruction. Other teaching programs in the church including women's Bible studies, marriage workshops, support groups, and sermons can also reinforce this message.

Ask the victim if she would be willing to speak to the minister or ask her permission to do so. Ministers trained in this area can provide counseling or make appropriate referrals. It is possible that the minister can counsel and exercise his authority with the husband; however, it is important to consider the safety and feelings of the victim. If the woman is afraid to make a move, encourage her to seek counseling at a specialized counseling center for battered women, so she can regain some sense of self-esteem and empowerment to make the necessary changes and leave the abusive situation.

Abusers can also benefit from counseling. Many abusers have issues that stem from their own background, which promote their abusive behaviors. They need to understand these issues and discover a better way of handling their feelings than resorting to abuse. It would be wise to refer such people to therapists trained in this specialized area.

3. When issues of immediate danger are involved, direct her to local sources of expertise in domestic violence. If needed, refer to a hospital emergency room for medical attention. There, injuries will be evaluated and documented along with information the victim conveys as to how they were received. Emergency rooms that follow good guidelines for domestic violence evaluation such as the one developed by the American Medical Association will train their staff to ask sensitively about domestic violence. This is suspected whenever there are injuries that do not appear to be accidental, especially if it does not match up to the story offered by the victim.

Sometimes the pattern of injuries or evidence of sexual abuse can be revealing. Delays in seeking care for significant injuries are also suspect. An overly protective spouse or one who never leaves the side of the patient may be a clue to the problem. Doctors are encouraged to interview patients in a confidential setting, without the presence of the spouse, if there is suspected abuse. The victim can choose this time to reveal the abuse. The doctor or hospital staff can then inquire if the victim would like assistance in pressing legal charges against the abuser.

Generally, a woman's sense of her own immediate danger should be taken as a realistic appraisal. Hence, the hospital staff should ask if the woman has friends or family with whom she can stay. If not, she should be referred to a shelter or a safe house. If none are available, temporary hospitalization for the injuries may be a good alternative while arrangements are being made. A caring individual can provide support for the battered woman, as she negotiates these challenging steps.

For information about shelters or safe houses, contact your local police department. There may be private as well as public facilities, which provide temporary shelter from danger and offer the victim some protection of their identity and location. If the victim is willing, have her contact the police department to determine what recourse she has to ensure safety for herself. If there is evidence of danger to any children in the household, child protective services must be called. Many professionals including hospital staff, ministers, teachers, and counselors are mandated by law to contact child protective services in cases of suspected threat to the children. Specific agencies designed to protect children in your locale can be obtained from the police department, schools, or hospitals.

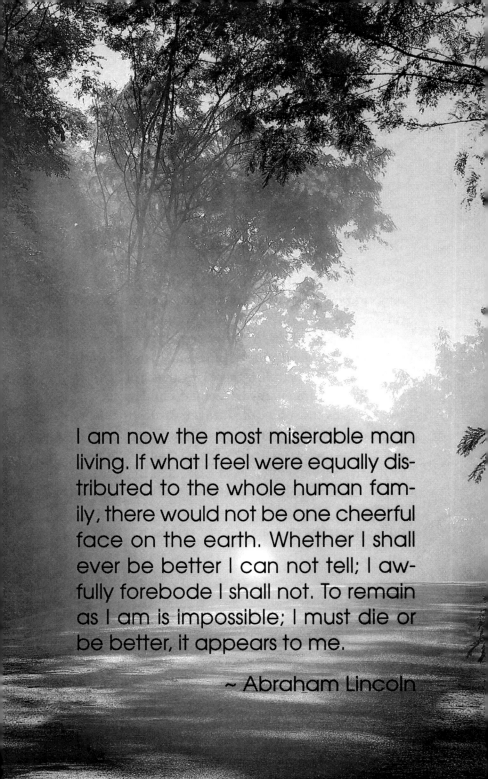

I am now the most miserable man living. If what I feel were equally distributed to the whole human family, there would not be one cheerful face on the earth. Whether I shall ever be better I can not tell; I awfully forebode I shall not. To remain as I am is impossible; I must die or be better, it appears to me.

~ Abraham Lincoln

CHAPTER 9

Depression
"An Illness, Not a Weakness"

L ILY IS A FORTY-NINE-YEAR-OLD CHURCH MEMBER WHO HAS always been active in the Ladies' Guild, serving in many capacities. She is a warm, friendly woman who often can be relied on to show hospitality to visiting missionaries as well as church members. She has always devoted herself to caring for her family. Her children are now young adults who are beginning to pursue lives of their own. One day Lily's daughter calls Maria, a friend of the family, and tells Maria that she is worried about her mother. It appears that Lily does not seem her usual cheerful self, and in fact, does not bother to get out of bed many mornings of the week. She also appears tired, withdrawn, and often bursts into tears unprovoked.

Maria gives Lily a call. When she explains the reason for her call and her concern, Lily seems somewhat embarrassed and states that nothing is really wrong. Lily was recently sick with the flu and thinks she is just tired. Maria agrees to pray for her, offering to help in any way she can. However, after hanging up, Maria does not feel she really connected with Lily.

A week later, Lily calls Maria and confesses that she is having problems with her family. She feels terribly anxious and irritable. Lily continues to talk about her family and how upset she is with them. Her friend listens patiently, asking questions occasionally. Lily finally admits, "I think there is something wrong with me."

Discussion

According to the National Institute of Mental Health, "In 2012, an estimated 16 million adults aged 18 or older in the U.S. had at least one major depressive episode in the past year. This represented 6.9 percent of all U.S. adults. Major depressive disorder is more prevalent in women than in men."[1]

Depression is often unrecognized and untreated. This is perhaps due to the stigma of having a mental health problem, which is unfortunate as there are many good treatments for depression.

The consequences of this disorder are major. Depression often impairs one's ability to perform at work, which may lead to job loss and prolonged unemployment. Disturbances in marital and family relationships can occur, and social and church relationships may be affected. Depressed persons are vulnerable to social isolation. Drug and alcohol abuse may result because depressed people may self-medicate to treat their terrible feelings. There may be increased physical complaints such as headaches, lethargy, and many other vague symptoms causing excessive visits to the medical doctor.

Recognizing the signs and symptoms of depression is the first step in meeting the challenges posed by this major health problem. The constellation of symptoms begins with almost constant depressed mood or irritability for at least a two-week period. In addition, there is often a sleep disturbance characterized by early morning awakening or multiple awakenings during the night.

Some complain that they sleep too much. Often there is a decrease in appetite with weight loss. However, in some people increased eating may occur, accompanied by weight gain. The depressed person often feels excessively tired and unable to concentrate. Some complain of intense anxiety or are worried about their physical health. Their thoughts may center on feelings of self-worthlessness, guilt that is often unrealistic, negative outlook on the future, and death. As a result, they may withdraw from their family and friends. They often lose their ability to enjoy things that were previously enjoyable. They may experience periods of spontaneous crying, although some depressed people describe an overwhelming sense of sadness but are unable to cry.

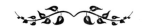

The Scriptures contain numerous examples of characters, some of them "heroes of the faith," who experienced depression, including Job, David, Elijah, Jonah, and Jacob.

One of the best biblical descriptions of depression is found in Psalm 88, attributed to Heman. Many of the symptoms of depression are described poignantly in this Psalm. Although not confirmed in the Psalm, some speculate that the writer may have suffered from leprosy. Nonetheless, Psalm 88 speaks of the feelings and thoughts of an afflicted individual, a sufferer who reveals his misery to God. This Psalm can be helpful to the suffering individual who can identify with the author, but it is by no means a cure. It is best used to assist loved ones and caregivers in understanding the mindset of the depressed individual. Understanding is a step toward empathy.

Lord, you are the God who saves me;
day and night I cry out to you.
May my prayer come before you;
turn your ear to my cry.
I am overwhelmed with troubles
and my life draws near to death.
I am counted among those who go down to the pit;
I am like one without strength.
I am set apart with the dead,
like the slain who lie in the grave,
whom you remember no more,
who are cut off from your care.
You have put me in the lowest pit,
in the darkest depths.
Your wrath lies heavily on me;
you have overwhelmed me with all your waves.
You have taken from me my closest friends
and have made me repulsive to them.
I am confined and cannot escape;
my eyes are dim with grief.
I call to you, Lord, every day;
I spread out my hands to you.
Do you show your wonders to the dead?
Do their spirits rise up and praise you?
Is your love declared in the grave,
your faithfulness in Destruction?
Are your wonders known in the place of darkness,
or your righteous deeds in the land of oblivion?
But I cry to you for help, Lord;
in the morning my prayer comes before you.
Why, Lord, do you reject me
and hide your face from me?
From my youth I have suffered and been close to death;
I have borne your terrors and am in despair.

Your wrath has swept over me;
your terrors have destroyed me.
All day long they surround me like a flood;
they have completely engulfed me.
You have taken from me friend and neighbor—
darkness is my closest friend.
Psalm 88:1-18

This psalmist describes many symptoms of depression.

- He cries out to the Lord day and night, indicating he is depressed.

- The fact that he does this day and night suggests insomnia.

- His "life draws near to death" suggests that his thoughts are centered around death.

- He reports excessive fatigue when he remarks that he is "like one without strength."

- His withdrawal from others is evident when he blames God for having "taken from me my closest friends."

- Anxiety is revealed when he claims that, "Your terrors have destroyed me."

These six symptoms of depression are fairly convincing if you are alert to them, so if your depressed friend agrees that he can identify with one or more of these, you might suggest that since depression like this is openly described in the Bible, it must be okay to reveal to others that we feel this way.

Additionally, you might ask the following questions:

- Do you have trouble concentrating?
- Do you feel tremendously guilty or worthless?

- Is your appetite disturbed?

- Do you find that nothing gives you any pleasure anymore?

According to the *Diagnostic and Statistical Manual of Mental Disorders, 5th Edition*, only five of the above symptoms are needed to make the diagnosis of clinical depression.[2] Yet it is remarkable how often the diagnosis is missed by peers and professionals. This may explain why the majority of depressions in this country are not treated.

Depression is a complex disorder that affects a person's entire life—physically, mentally, relationally, and spiritually. Thankfully, depression responds to treatment in most cases.

Because depression can wreak such havoc in all areas of a person's life, it is important to pursue treatment. Overcoming the stigma and ignorance surrounding depression is a challenge to both secular and church communities. One needs to overcome false ideas such as, "The person is depressed because he does not have enough faith." This can be damaging as the depressed person already has a propensity for excessive guilt and would easily be convinced that his faith is inadequate. Rather, he or she should be encouraged to seek help, much in the way that if one had pneumonia or diabetes one would seek medical attention. Many depressions are just as biologically based as pneumonia or diabetes.

Similarly false is the notion that depression is a direct result of excessive personal sinning. When a person appears to be suffering from depression, it is generally counterproductive to suggest that the depression is a punishment for sin. The counseling Job received from his friends is an example of such misleading interpretation. Depressed people will often unnecessarily take the blame, express repentance for some unknown sin, and then venture no further to seek help. They remain unaware of the biological basis of depression.

Brain chemicals such as serotonin and norepinephrine have been found to be disturbed in clinical depression. That is why for some patients, correcting these brain chemicals with medications such as escitalopram (Lexapro), sertraline (Zoloft), venlafaxine (Effexor), bupropion (Wellbutrin), nortriptyline (Pamelor), fluoxetine (Prozac), and others can dramatically improve the depression. It also explains why some depressions have a familial tendency and that for some reason some people are genetically vulnerable to depression just like others are genetically predisposed to migraines, which can occur and recur under conditions of stress or spontaneously. Because clinical depression does not manifest itself in visible symptoms such as a rash, or a finding such as an elevated blood pressure, or in an abnormal blood test, many find it difficult to recognize depression when it occurs. The manifestations are largely in thought processes and behavior, which serves to disguise its biological origins. It is labeled as "emotional," without understanding that many emotional symptoms have biological causes.

There are various sources of help for the depressed individual. A consultation with a specially trained physician such as a psychiatrist can determine the presence of clinical depression. Other professionals such as psychologists, trained social workers, and counselors with expertise in evaluating depression may provide needed information. If medication is required only a medical doctor can prescribe it. A family physician can be consulted for two reasons. One is to make sure that the person's physical examination is normal and that he does not have a medical illness that mimics depression, and the other reason is to obtain a referral to the appropriate mental health professional in the community. Clergymen may have information about local physicians and other professionals whom they recommend. When these are not available, medical centers and hospital psychiatric departments may be helpful through their referral network.

In addition, Christian organizations such as Focus On the Family maintain a counseling department, which provides information and referrals from their extensive registry of Christian counseling professionals throughout the United States. They can be reached at the address and telephone number printed in the resource section at the end of this book. Also, the American Psychiatric Association which is based in Washington, D.C., has district branches which may provide listings of board certified psychiatrists. See the resource listing at the end of this book for address and telephone.

Lily's condition may seem vague and unclear on first look. But on closer inspection, there are clues to her depression such as spontaneous crying, irritability, anxiety, withdrawal, tiredness, and even her own determination that, "There's something wrong with me." All this should be taken seriously. From a spiritual point of view, sufferers require reassurance that although they may be preoccupied with an overwhelming sense of guilt and weakness from the depression, their God would carry them through this trial just as He would any other. The goal is to facilitate their getting appropriate help in order to take care of the body and mind that God has given them. In order not to place a judgment value on the condition it is important to remember: "Depression is an illness, not a weakness."[3]

A special type of depression warrants description. This is called major depression with peripartum onset[4] or more familiarly known as "postpartum depression." Depression can start during pregnancy and then extend into the postpartum period. Because it is frequently unrecognized and therefore untreated, the following illustration is presented to provide a greater understanding of this condition.

Mr. Questra, a first time father, appears at your door, looking weary and haggard and asks to speak to you concerning his wife. He relates that Mrs. Questra has just berated him miserably and asked him to leave the house. Complaining that he was lazy and unhelpful with their newborn, that he did not complete all the preparations necessary for the baby's arrival, and that he was inattentive and insensitive to her feelings, she broke out into fits of sobbing and demanded that he leave. Mr. Questra was confused. He had never seen his wife this way and sought out his pastor for help.

Three weeks ago, after a difficult delivery, Mrs. Questra gave birth to a normal, healthy girl. She thought it was strange that she did not feel as joyful about the event as she had anticipated. In fact, she noticed that she was very anxious about the baby's health, her own health, and preoccupied with these thoughts all the time. Nighttime was dreadful as she ruminated over fears about whether she was a good mother and whether the baby's crying meant that there was something terribly wrong. Insomnia plagued her daily, and she could not eat as her stomach was "tied in knots" from worry.

Mr. Questra tried very hard to help his wife, but she did not seem to notice or appreciate his efforts. He took time off from his job and even obtained around the clock help from his sisters. Nothing seemed to cheer or distract his wife. He was at his wits end.

You decide to visit the couple at their home the next day, and after an initial awkward silence, Mrs. Questra becomes distracted by the baby's cry. She appears very uncomfortable and exclaims that she is unfit to be a mother.

The experts indicate that depression around the time of pregnancy is common, stating "Although the estimates differ according to the period of follow-up after delivery, between 3% and 6% of women will experience the onset of a major depressive episode during pregnancy or in the weeks or months following delivery."[5] This condition is often not recognized when it occurs in the church community. Yet it is a common illness that occurs in the life of a woman. It causes tremendous emotional pain in the mother, which can negatively affect mother-infant bonding and may lead to impaired cognitive development of the child. It often wreaks havoc on the marital relationship as well as impacting other children in the family.

Recognizing the presence of peripartum depression is extremely important. Many should share in this responsibility, including the affected woman, doctors, nurses, childbirth educators, family members, and also the church community. The latter represents a large circle of concerned individuals who may have had similar experiences and may be able to share in the new mother's psychological support and spiritual encouragement. They can also prompt each other to seek treatment when necessary. In addition, they can provide assistance with childcare responsibilities while the mother is afflicted.

What are the symptoms of a peripartum depression? First, one needs to distinguish "depression" from "postpartum blues," which is a temporary condition after childbirth, and not the same as clinical depression. Postpartum blues usually last for a few days after delivery and is characterized by crying spells, irritability, and mood instability. This condition is assumed to result from the rapid hormonal changes after birth. Its key feature is that it resolves spontaneously after a few days.

On the other hand, postpartum and peripartum depression represent a persistent depressed mood lasting for two weeks or longer. During this time, the woman is depressed most of the day, and there is a loss of pleasure. In addition, she may suffer from insomnia (even when the baby is sleeping), change in appetite (significant increase or decrease), anxiety regarding her own health or the welfare of the child, fatigue, or recurrent thoughts of death. An unusual form of depression that represents a psychiatric emergency occurs when the woman also experiences a break with reality demonstrated by auditory or visual hallucinations or delusions. The latter may include thoughts such as "the child is possessed by the devil." Immediate psychiatric attention and often hospitalization is warranted as both the child and the mother are at risk because of the mother's delusional perceptions. This condition is called psychosis.

Risk factors for peripartum depression include a previous history of depression (peripartum or non-peripartum), family history of depression or alcoholism, poor early childhood environment, unwanted pregnancy, a complicated labor and delivery, poor obstetrical outcome (birth defects), or marital discord. If these factors exist, timely counseling and support should be obtained.

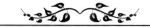

Support groups provide a sense of mutual validation for shared feelings and experiences. It helps to know that someone else understands and cares.

However, many women develop peripartum depression even without risk factors. Therefore, if these symptoms develop they should be encouraged to pursue treatment immediately.

Treatment is effective in peripartum depression and often includes using anti-depressant medication, individual psychotherapy, marital or family counseling, or group support. In some cases, hospitalization, antipsychotic medication, or electro-convulsive treatments may be needed. Because treatments are effective and the consequences of untreated depression are major, women should be encouraged to seek help to relieve the distress of this debilitating condition.

How People Can Help

The church can be instrumental in helping the mother with peripartum depression. It can provide a strong network of support for these suffering women until they regain their emotional health.

1. Supporting the mother: Assist the mother in getting professional help if she has not done so yet. Generally, depression responds well to medication treatment so a psychiatrist would be a good choice for obtaining care. The obstetrician should be told of any symptoms described above at the postpartum check-up, which generally occurs six weeks after birth. He or she can be a good referral source for psychiatric attention.

   Provide ample babysitting for the mother as needed. She will need time for herself either to rest or simply to attend to her own needs. Certain antidepressant medications may be sedating, so help for the care of the baby needs to be arranged. Keep in mind that there needs to be a balance between providing extra help in caring for the baby and encouraging mother-infant bonding.

   One common characteristic of peripartum depression is intense anxiety experienced by the mother. She is often overwhelmed by concerns over the welfare of the child and her own health. The mother is plagued with a great deal of doubt about herself and her mothering ability. Women who have gone through this process can provide reassurance to the new mother.

2. The church can provide ongoing support groups for young mothers. Being the mother of an infant or young children can be a stressful and isolating experience. It is worse for those women who suffer from peripartum depression. The church community has the resources to diminish these burdensome conditions by providing

opportunities for young mothers to meet on a regular basis. Their identified purposes for meeting can center on multiple themes such as Bible study, prayer meeting, weekly luncheons, or educational workshops. The latter should incorporate topics relevant to young mothers such as Christian parenting, the healthy marriage, understanding relationships, the role of prayer, overcoming depression, or any other issue that is relevant to the members of the group.

To facilitate these groups, many topical study guides and Bible study aids for women's groups have been published. They can be used to stimulate discussion and learning. Furthermore, besides education, these groups provide the intangible elements that are therapeutic in any group process. A group setting may provide the participants with a sense of support and mutual validation for shared feelings and experiences. The group process removes the sense of isolation and provides an extended family of adult members, mutually caring for each other. Weekly meetings also provide a needed sense of structure to the week that is necessary to combat the often frenzied nature of raising young children. Ideally, these groups should be coordinated by someone who is trained or sensitive to the needs of young mothers. The leader should make an effort to provide consistency in meeting. This is often difficult to do when the demands of a young mother's life may make it impossible for her regular attendance. The pragmatic matter of childcare should be arranged so that mothers can have a much needed and possibly rare opportunity to participate in adult conversation and stimulation.

Many secular support groups have been established in various communities throughout the country. Women with peripartum depression discover that they are not alone as they learn more about their condition. When needed, church groups can borrow from the information and experiences offered by these postpartum depression support groups. Women who have recovered from depression provide strong encouragement to new mothers. The groups can be easily established in the church setting. Women's fellowships or group meetings for young mothers can address many of these issues, which affect new mothers. These groups can provide emotional and spiritual support.

3. Support the father and the family. All family members suffer when a woman develops peripartum depression. The father needs support, both practical help and emotional comfort, while he attends to the multiple new demands required of him. The church can offer help in many of these matters, whether it is assistance with overwhelming household chores, cooking, etc.

A wife's peripartum depression leaves a new father very confused. Having a baby is usually anticipated with much joy, and when quite the opposite occurs, the father may not be able to fathom the problem. Appropriate help and counseling from the minister or other church members can mobilize the father into getting the needed professional help for his wife.

If there are other siblings in the home, the church can help by attending to their needs. Often the care of siblings can be overlooked when a mother has peripartum depression, and church members can assist where there are temporary lapses in caring for siblings.

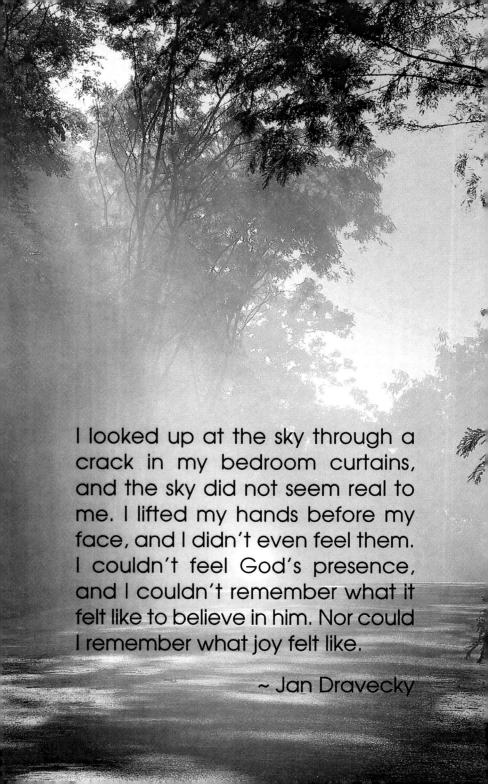

I looked up at the sky through a crack in my bedroom curtains, and the sky did not seem real to me. I lifted my hands before my face, and I didn't even feel them. I couldn't feel God's presence, and I couldn't remember what it felt like to believe in him. Nor could I remember what joy felt like.

~ Jan Dravecky

CHAPTER 10

Premenstrual Dysphoric Disorder

*I*RIS IS A TWENTY-EIGHT-YEAR-OLD WOMAN WHO IS ONE OF THE choir members in a church. She is usually cheerful, friendly, and enjoys singing very much. The people that know her find that while she seems very contented, there are times when she seems quite stressed, tired, and nervous. Her friendly manner is replaced by withdrawal and a lack of energy. One day in choir, after the conductor remarks that she seems tired, she snaps at him and yells, "If you had to worry about what I had to today, you'd be tired, too."

Iris apologizes for her abruptness and seems quite agitated. She later tells a friend in the choir that lately she has been feeling irritable and anxious each month. In addition, she has always had trouble with being overweight, but recently, she has noticed that none of her clothes fit. Her feet and fingers are swollen, and she just feels miserable.

At the next rehearsal, she seems her usual cheerful self. She and her friend are both excitedly talking about the upcoming performance of Handel's Messiah for the special Christmas service, and they have both been given challenging solos. They plan to get together and rehearse their parts on a weekly basis. Even though it is hard work, over the weeks that follow, Iris makes great progress on the solo, and both she and her friend can see that Iris is gifted with a special talent. In fact, the entire choir is at the height of perfection with just two weeks left to the performance. All the choir members, including Iris, are thankful and joyful at being able to serve God in song. Two days later, the phone rings, and Iris is on the line crying, telling her friend that she feels she cannot sing in the upcoming performance. She wants to know whether her friend can take her place.

> This condition can be challenging to deal with, both for the woman affected and those who care about her. A partnership of discerning friends and physicians can help.

Discussion

Premenstrual syndrome (PMS) has been defined in many ways and is used to describe the mood, behavioral, and physical symptoms that occur in some women during the week prior to menstruation. This phase is called the "late luteal phase." During this time many women experience symptoms ranging from a single mild symptom to having a collection of symptoms severe enough to cause problems in function. Or their PMS may interfere with their social relationships. These symptoms should end just after the onset of the menstrual period.

A severe form of PMS exists and is called "Premenstrual Dysphoric Disorder" (PMDD).[1] The criteria states that a woman should experience symptoms in the week prior to her period with resolution after it is over for nearly every cycle in the past year. These symptoms must add up to five of the following, and require one from the following four:

- anger/irritability,
- depressed/sad mood,
- anxiety/feeling tense,
- experiencing labile mood (rapid changes in mood from sad to happy in a short period of time).

Other symptoms include:

- a change in appetite or certain food cravings,
- sleep disturbance,
- tiredness,
- feelings of being overwhelmed,
- poor concentration,
- various physical complaints including bloating, breast tenderness, or joint pains.

These symptoms are severe enough to impair a woman's ability to function and should be distinguished from other psychiatric conditions such as clinical depression, anxiety disorders, or other medical disorders. The diagnosis has to be confirmed by two months of testing using a daily rating form.

Only a small percentage of women actually have PMDD. It is important for women to seek help in identifying whether they have PMDD or another psychiatric condition that can be treated. Premenstrual symptoms can also be addressed through a number of other ways, including lifestyle changes. Women will benefit from proper exercise. Exercise increases bodily chemicals called "endorphins," which improves a person's sense of well-being. Although it may not cure PMS, it certainly will help the mood changes that some women experience during the premenstrual week.

Proper nutrition is also important. Decreasing dietary intake of salt will help cut down on fluid retention and the symptom of bloating. Caffeine restriction may also be helpful in reducing breast discomfort. Managing stress in the premenstrual week is an important strategy. For example, if a woman has some control over her schedule, she can choose to perform less stressful tasks during the premenstrual week. The effectiveness of vitamin supplementation is controversial. However, women do utilize them. Dr. Mary Jane Minkin, a gynecologist with the Yale University Medical College, writes that she has recommended vitamin B6, vitamin E, and a health supplement called "evening primrose oil" for PMS. She has found that they have been helpful in many cases.[2] Other treatments include various hormonal regimens, which should be discussed with a gynecologist. Diuretics are sometimes used to treat bloating, but a physician should monitor this to prevent disturbing the body's potassium supply. Calcium supplementation may also be helpful. Finally for premenstrual dysphoric disorder, there are antidepressants called selective serotonin reuptake inhibitors (SSRIs) such as fluoxetine (Prozac) and sertraline (Zoloft), which are effective.

Dr. Anna L. Stout, of Duke University Medical Center, reported on a research project involving twelve academic centers, which studied 234 women with the diagnosis of PMDD. The study showed that sertraline (Zoloft) was significantly more effective than a placebo in the treatment of these women.[3] Patients with a family history or a previous personal history of depression with PMS should consider obtaining a psychiatric evaluation for depression and the possible use of an antidepressant.

Treatment of underlying psychiatric conditions is also important in order to relieve some symptoms that are exacerbated within the premenstrual period. For example, if a woman suffers from panic disorder and she is more anxious premenstrually, she may attribute her panic attacks to PMS. It is also important that clinical depression be distinguished from PMS. If a woman's PMS lasts for several weeks per month, it is not PMS but more likely something else such as depression. It is important to discern this as there are effective treatments for depression. A proper evaluation by a gynecologist or a psychiatrist who specializes in the areas of PMS will provide a diagnosis. A well-integrated approach including psychiatric and gynecologic care as well as lifestyle improvements are recommended.

Iris' case is typical of many women who have premenstrual symptoms. She experiences abdominal bloating such that her clothes do not fit. She generally seems well but then surprisingly becomes irritable, snappy, tired, and anxious about not just her routine but about a singing engagement that she has clearly mastered. The anxiety in the premenstrual week has changed her perception of her abilities by making her anxious. Iris does bring her complaints to her gynecologist and finds that she has a normal gynecologic examination. She then sees the psychiatrist referred by her gynecologist, and soon a diagnosis is made. Iris has PMDD. In the past, she has had clinical depressions, which have never been treated. Medication and counseling are provided. She begins to learn more about her condition and makes the necessary changes in her life. It should not be surprising that she goes on to sing the Hallelujah chorus with confidence and excellence.

Proper diagnosis and medical treatment for PMDD, coupled with appropriate lifestyle adjustments, can help control the more problematic symptoms of this disorder.

How People Can Help

1. The church community can offer vital assistance in the lifestyle changes that work for women who suffer from premenstrual syndrome. General rules of good health such as exercise, proper nutrition, and limitation of the use of agents such as alcohol, caffeine, salt, and fat can be integrated into a program designed for women. Such a program can take the form of a regular exercise group meeting at the church, integrated with educational workshops. The underlying philosophy of the group should be taking care of oneself as a form of proper stewardship of the body that God has given each woman. Hence, biblical study and support can be offered to motivate the members to continue in the proper care of their bodies. When such a program is effective, it offers women mutual support, accountability to each other in maintaining disciplined exercise, and the opportunity to share health information.

   An example of this type of program is Body and Soul Fitness, which has developed an exercise program that can be utilized in any church setting. It is designed for use by Christian women. The program has established numerous expertly designed aerobics classes throughout different Christian settings in the country. They have developed a training program and materials including videotapes, CDs and manuals, which provide ongoing instruction for the exercise class and its leader. Combining the scriptural teaching which is drawn from the music that is used for the exercises as well as the Bible, the Body and Soul Fitness has combined a program of good physical as well as spiritual health. Advocates of the program have testified to its positive effect on physical well-being, mood, as well as on the management of chronic illnesses such as diabetes mellitus. Certainly, it will also benefit those women suffering from PMS. For more information, please refer to the resource section at the end of this book. Health education is an important tool and can be disseminated in the church setting, whether it be done in women's groups or provided in publications. In the field of PMDD, there are many different treatments that have been offered as well as new developments in both the self-help and medical arenas.

If you are suffering from PMDD or you know someone who is, try to learn as much as you can about PMDD, depression, and anxiety disorders. You can obtain information from books, magazines, individuals in the medical or mental health field, and even from patients who have been successfully treated. Being well informed is one way you can be of help to the women in your church.

2. Encouragement is a tool for handling PMS. Because of the cyclical nature of PMDD, women can quickly appreciate that there are days in the month when anxiety, down mood, or physical tension can affect their perceptions of their own performance and life in general. They also can recognize that these conditions resolve with the onset of menses. Women can help each other by reminding each other that the mood symptoms will abate and that they will soon be back to their usual selves. When possible, they can assist each other by sharing responsibilities. Most importantly, the psychological support offered by women to other women is invaluable.

3. Caring church members can help women who are debilitated by their premenstrual symptoms by suggesting professional or medical intervention. It is useful to know the

differences between professional resources when you refer someone for help. Gynecologists are medical doctors who are expert in the biology of the female reproductive system and therefore can evaluate whether there is anything physically wrong. A psychiatrist is also a medical doctor who can determine whether mood changes that may be attributed to PMS, might be the result of a treatable mental condition such as depression or anxiety disorder. They can provide medication as well as psychotherapy (talk therapy) and counseling. Psychologists, social workers, and psychotherapists generally are trained to provide different forms of counseling and talk therapy. They do not prescribe medications but some may work in collaboration with a psychiatrist when medication is needed.

4. Sufferers play a unique role in helping other sufferers. This is described in the following Scripture passage.

> *Praise be to the God and Father of our Lord Jesus Christ,*
> *the Father of compassion and the God of all comfort,*
> *who comforts us in all our troubles, so that we can*
> *comfort those in any trouble with the comfort*
> *we ourselves receive from God.*
> 2 Corinthians 1:3-4

Those individuals who have suffered and recovered from a mental illness represent a great resource of information, experience, and testimony to those who are afflicted for the first time. The Christian who has had experience with depression, anxiety disorders, or premenstrual dysphoric disorder has learned many lessons and facts about the process of recovery that would be of vital encouragement to those who need to travel a similar route. These lessons can be communicated to facilitate the journey. For example, a Christian who has recovered from mental illness can tell the sufferer that he or she can view treatment and/or medication as tools that God has provided for the healing of the sufferer. He can teach the sufferer that having a mental illness is not a result of sin, as many are apt to believe, but rather, like all disease processes, the result of living in an imperfect world with imperfect bodies.

Where treatments exist, one should take advantage of these and Christians can thank God for them. Christian sufferers who have recovered can gently guide others through the maze of treatment seeking. And most importantly, they provide the comfort to those who are suffering by communicating to them that they are not alone, that these problems do occur among Christians, and that they are the evidence that they can be overcome.

While the ability of sufferers to help other sufferers is valid and important across all mental illnesses, why include it in a chapter on PMS? There are two reasons. First, PMDD is a uniquely woman's issue, at least from a biological perspective. Many women feel comfortable in talking to and confiding with other women about health problems and perhaps to a lesser degree about mental health issues. Whether it be in a group forum in church or in a quiet conversation between two women, many mental health symptoms and difficult-to-talk-about concerns are shared.

In recent years, it has become easier for women to talk about their PMS openly. Partly through improved health education in the media and partly because it seems so widespread, women do not find it as stigmatizing to talk about their monthly symptoms. In fact, many women will readily go to the doctor for help with their PMS while remaining averse to seeking a medical consultation for depression or another mental illness. Ironically, because the symptoms of PMS are similar to psychiatric conditions, these women discover that what they really have is a clinical depression or an anxiety disorder. If this occurs, and they are directed to the appropriate treatment, they will benefit from receiving the proper diagnosis.

This leads to the second reason why the notion of PMDD represents an opportunity for recovered sufferers to help others. Premenstrual syndrome is often the diagnosis women make about themselves when what they really have may be an exacerbation of medical or psychiatric conditions including endometriosis, pelvic inflammatory disease, clinical depression, eating disorders, and finally anxiety disorders. A physician can make the appropriate determination. There is also some evidence to support the fact that a subgroup of women who have premenstrual dysphoric disorder resemble but do not meet the full criteria for depression, yet do respond to antidepressants. In any case, women choose to use PMS as a description for symptoms of other conditions, which are exacerbated premenstrually. Only consultation with a thorough physician insures proper diagnosis.

It is incumbent upon thoughtful friends and caring family to help uncover these mistakes and direct women to the proper help. Women who have labeled their symptoms as PMS and then been found to have depression or anxiety disorders can help educate their peers with sensitivity. That is to say, they understand the need to label symptoms with the neutral title of PMS while at the same time be able to help look for the real underlying condition. They have learned to discern when PMS is *not* PMS. For example, PMS is not PMS when the woman notes symptoms for more than two weeks out of every month. This is too long a period to be truly premenstrual. It is not PMS when her only "good week" is not that good relative to her usual self. In other words, if she is depressed or anxious all month but much more so during the week prior to menses, this does not support the diagnosis of PMS.

It is not PMS when a woman is totally incapacitated or suicidal. It is far better to look for other treatable causes of these conditions. It cannot be called PMS if the woman is taking oral contraceptives simply because contraceptives prevent ovulation and the hormonal events that create a normal menstrual cycle. While a doctor would make the definitive diagnosis after evaluation, women who have suffered from these conditions can help their peers sort out their symptoms just by the sharing of information.

The process by which a recovered sufferer helps another, whether it is in the area of premenstrual dysphoric disorder or other psychiatric illnesses, requires a certain amount of self-revelation. Clearly, when it is done in a timely and appropriate manner, it is helpful. Support groups for the various illnesses have testified to the benefit of mutual support, health education, self-help, and professional attention. This type of support can occur on an individual level from one sufferer to another. However, this is not an argument for total self-revelation without discernment. There are advantages and drawbacks, which again relate to the stigmatization that comes from societal ignorance in relation to those who have a mental illness. There are also individual circumstances and factors to consider. Hence, self-revelation must be an individualized decision and ultimately a choice.

When one person reveals information about herself to help another, ideally this should be met with respect and gratitude. The person has risked his or her privacy and potential stigmatization to help educate another. In the best scenario, there would be mutual benefit. In conclusion, sharing of experiences and testimonies prove that these scenarios are happening all the time in various church communities. People privately help one another through life experiences that often are not talked about in public. This should be applauded.

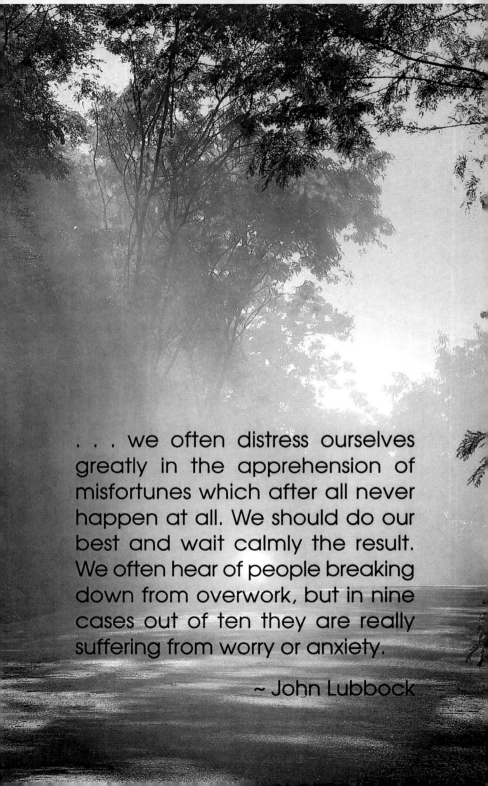

. . . we often distress ourselves greatly in the apprehension of misfortunes which after all never happen at all. We should do our best and wait calmly the result. We often hear of people breaking down from overwork, but in nine cases out of ten they are really suffering from worry or anxiety.

~ John Lubbock

CHAPTER 11

Obsessions and Compulsions

MARIANNE, A MIDDLE-AGED SCHOOLTEACHER, WORSHIPPED in a large church in a metropolitan area. She was quite active in her church, working in the areas of evangelism and ministries to the homeless. She enjoyed a successful career as a schoolteacher and the respect of her fellow church members in her ability to teach Sunday school, to organize activities, and to be of encouragement to those who are suffering. Little did anyone know, Marianne was suffering as well.

Marianne had always known that she had quirky, eccentric ways since she was a child. She would often be bound to certain "habits" such as "not stepping on a crack because I'll break my parent's back." Although many children play this game, Marianne's mother always felt that her daughter took it to an extreme. Marianne would refuse to veer from this rule and was often late getting to school. When her mother tried to force her to change, she would become very anxious and upset. She also had to have her toys organized symmetrically or she would not be comfortable. Although Marianne did reasonably well in school earning top grades and developing a few friends, she remained quite an anxious child and was fearful of new situations. After marriage, she blossomed and became very active socially and in her church.

The pastor always welcomed Marianne into his committee meetings. She had a flair and an enthusiasm for the Lord's work that seemed to encourage him when he felt somewhat discouraged. One day Marianne approached him to discuss her fears about a particular church project. She told him that she was worried the program might not get under way without the help of a large number of people and that she felt doubtful about her ability to handle the task. She hinted that she was constantly praying in order to get direction from God but felt she wasn't getting answers no matter how hard she prayed. She felt quite anxious and hoped that she could meet again with the pastor on this matter.

At the next meeting, Marianne, though never a prompt person, arrived quite late and apologized, saying that she could not get out of the house on time, vaguely mumbling that there was so much to do. She presented a long list of items that needed to be done on the project and remarked that she had worked all week on this list checking and rechecking it for its completeness. The pastor looked at it and pondered. This project although important, did not warrant the kind of worry and scrutiny that Marianne seemed to give it. In addition, the list, although adequate, did not reflect the number of hours that Marianne had poured into it. He thanked her for her work and puzzled over her overanxious manner.

One day, the pastor was surprised to see Marianne's husband at his office. The husband asked if he might speak to the pastor about his wife. He explained that he was concerned and frustrated with his wife's behavior. She was constantly working on this church project, making lists and lists but didn't seem to get anywhere. In addition, she would check the lists so much before going out to church or to work that they would be constantly late for activities. He admitted that his wife had always been a "checker" and a "worrier," repeatedly checking the stove and the locks to the door. Sometimes the husband could distract her from repeatedly doing this, but now he had grown quite exasperated with her.

The new obsession over the church project was the last straw. She was constantly talking to him about the plans until he was sick of it. She would call everybody on the committee and repeat her concerns to the point where her husband felt she might be alienating the members. But his biggest complaint was that she spent so much time checking and praying over her lists that

> Sometimes Marianne spent so much time checking and rechecking and praying and re-praying over her lists that nothing else actually was accomplished.

nothing else was being done in the house. He really felt bad about all this because he could see when he confronted his wife that she was very sorry, but she did not know how to stop. She seemed compelled to do all this and when she tried to stop and attend to other matters, she became even more anxious. She was now constantly late for work, church, and all social activities. The pastor consoled the husband and offered to speak to Marianne. After praying together, the husband thanked the pastor for his help.

The next Sunday, the pastor approached Marianne and explained what he had learned from her husband. Marianne, at first looked very troubled but then with a sigh of relief and resignation admitted, "I know this is ridiculous, and I know I have to break out of this, but I am just at a loss." She then turned her head toward him and in a desperate and defeated manner asked, "Pastor, can you help me?"

Discussion

How does one respond to this plea for help? If one is not acquainted with Marianne's condition, it will be difficult to know what to say. Some hunt for spiritual explanations for this malady. Others will offer speculations based on their understanding of emotional issues. In the area of pastoral counseling, there is often an expectation for the clergyman to have an explanation for all that befalls man. However, proverbial wisdom teaches, "An honest answer is like a kiss on the lips" (Prov. 24:26). Sometimes, the humility expressed in the admission, "I don't know much about what you are going through, but I will try to help you get the answers," paves the road for successful pastoral intervention.

Obsessive compulsive disorder (OCD) is the diagnosis for Marianne's condition. This disorder is often unrecognized, and sufferers tend to keep their problems secret. The hallmarks of this condition are the presence of obsessions and/or compulsions. Obsessions are repetitive, intrusive thoughts, urges, or images that plague a person's mind. These obsessions are experienced as distressing and inappropriate. Adults with OCD will generally recognize that these obsessions are excessive and unrealistic. Children with OCD may not be able to make such a determination and thus believe their obsessive thoughts.

Compulsions are defined as repeated behaviors that attempt to quell the anxiety generated by the obsessions.[1] For example, a person such as Marianne may have performed the repetitive checking behaviors in response to some intrusive obsession such as, "If I don't check my lists, the stove, or the locks, something terrible will happen." Marianne recognizes that this is an unrealistic and irrational pattern of thought, but she will find that it will continue to recur and cause her to be a slave to her compulsive checking. Obsessive-compulsive disorder causes a major disturbance in people's ability to function in their occupational life as well as their daily routine. They may find that these repetitive thoughts and acts are time-consuming. The thoughts and acts can take up hours each day of their time and progress to the point where the person cannot function normally. Often, the degree of stress on one's mental life can cause significant problems with a person's ability to concentrate on academic or job responsibilities and may affect their relationships. In the worst case scenario, a person can be virtually housebound, as in the case of Marianne.

Marianne's obsessions and compulsions take up all her time, rendering her unable to perform her job, participate in her church ministry, take care of her home, or even personal hygiene. In many patients, it can lead to a clinical depression. There are a variety of obsessions and compulsions that can affect a person's life. The most common obsessions include a fear of contamination, a fear that one has left something undone, and pathological doubt about oneself, or a situation involving oneself. Upsetting sexual thoughts or images, intrusive thoughts of violence, or excessive worry that one has inadvertently hurt someone are also frequent. Inexplicable anxiety may also occur for some people if objects are not in a certain order, whether it be symmetrically or numerically determined. There are also many forms of obsessions that are idiosyncratic and individualistic. No matter how unusual the obsessions or compulsions, they all share the feature that they are distressing, causing anxiety, and recognized as being intrusive and inappropriate by the OCD sufferer.

Repetitive compulsions, whether they are behaviors or repeated mental activities, are performed in order to quell the anxiety generated by the obsession. These would include compulsions to repeatedly wash one's hands if one has a marked fear of contamination or repeated checking rituals. Other compulsive behaviors include counting rituals, repeating certain phrases, and idiosyncratic placement of objects without veering from the "required" pattern. These manifestations of OCD are common to non-Christians as well as Christians suffering from this disorder. Like obsessions, compulsions can take on many different forms in different individuals.

In Marianne's case, she had a repeated need to check her lists to look for things that she felt she might have left undone. She also checked her stove and locks constantly, not being satisfied that she had already checked. However, she had a number of compulsions that may not be recognized as such because they appear to fit into the perceived norms of the Christian life. An example of this is compulsive praying in response to an obsession. Although Christians recognize that praying is an important part of their spiritual life, compulsive praying is excessive, prolonged, and despite its time consumption does not quell the anxiety caused by the obsession. After treatment, many Christians recognize the difference between genuine, faithful praying, and obsessional praying.

Other manifestations of OCD among Christians may include pathologic doubt regarding one's salvation or doubt about one's ability to be forgiven. This is called "scrupulosity," which entails having a false sense of guilt and a perception that one has done something wrong, even when there is no evidence for it. It can include doubts regarding one's spiritual life. One can imagine the complexities involved in discerning between acceptance of the doctrine of the sinful nature of man versus the manifestations of scrupulosity in OCD.

One point of distinction is that Christians with OCD will find it difficult to draw expected comfort from scriptural promises if they are in opposition to their obsessive worry. For example, someone who has pathological doubt regarding their personal salvation would have trouble believing the personal application of John 3:16, "For God so loved the world that he gave his one and only Son, that whoever believes in him shall not perish but have eternal life." They often question themselves regarding their Christian status. And despite repeated recitation of scriptural promises by loved ones, they remain doubtful about truths such as stated in 1 John 1:9, "If we confess our sins, he is faithful and just and will forgive us our sins and purify us from all unrighteousness." This pathologic doubt robs a Christian of peace and joy and may interfere with ministries that they had been quite capable of performing when they were not afflicted.

Almost any aspect of religious life can be incorporated into obsessions and compulsions. Therefore, it is important for Christians to recognize when they or a family member is suffering from OCD. Dr. Bruce Ballard, of Cornell University Medical College states, "Activities that seem so deviant from the norm of those who are intensely religious are clues to the possibility of underlying emotional disturbance. This is the model one uses to ascertain whether certain behaviors fit within a person's cultural background or would be viewed as abnormal by others within the culture."[2]

Many cases are not recognized as the obsessions are often kept secret and the compulsions are often not done in public. As a result, the individual may withdraw from his peers as he is consumed by the obsessions and compulsions, leaving most to wonder what happened. Even in Marianne's case, family members may not fully understand the psychological processes that cause this disturbing condition.

Sometimes Christians with OCD cannot apply scriptural truth to themselves; as in, "God may love the whole world, but He surely cannot love a wretched sinner like me!"

Nevertheless, individuals suffer a great deal of anguish when they experience obsessions and compulsions. This is made worse by the fact that they recognize that their thoughts are inappropriate. They are intensely embarrassed and ashamed of their thoughts and therefore suffer in silence.

Many patients with OCD demonstrate a waxing and waning course during their lifetime with periods of exacerbation, which can occur spontaneously or under times of life stress. A small percentage develop a downhill course in their ability to function at work or socially. In the past generation, there have been many advances in the treatment of OCD. Effective medications include fluoxetine (Prozac), escitalopram (Lexapro), sertraline (Zoloft), and paroxetine (Paxil). These drugs work to regulate a chemical in the brain called serotonin, which goes awry in OCD. Once the medication is started, it may be several weeks before some improvement is noted. When it happens, many patients report that the intrusiveness of the thoughts diminishes or they find them less distressing. Psychological treatments are designed to assist the patient in controlling his compulsions and coping with his obsessions.

A person with OCD needs to learn various ways of halting his intrusive thoughts, e.g. "thought stopping." Some find that snapping a rubber band on the wrist when they experience the intrusive thoughts may help prevent the obsession from taking hold. Others try to visualize a big "STOP" sign. Still others may find distraction a help to get away from the obsession. It is important that sufferers seek treatment from professionals to learn important coping tools that work best for them.

Compulsions, which result from obsessive thoughts, such as checking behaviors, can also be approached. Generally, a person can practice curbing compulsions by continually exposing himself to situations that may promote obsessive thinking, while preventing himself from giving in to performing the compulsion. Eventually, he will learn to tolerate the anxiety of not performing the compulsion and the anxiety will decrease with time and practice. These techniques result in less time spent on compulsive behaviors and improved ability to function. There has been increased public awareness about the frequency of OCD and its diagnosis. Because there are effective treatments, people like Marianne have the potential to obtain relief from their symptoms. Education and emotional support is needed to help them know that their obsessions are unrealistic and that they can develop the means to resume their lives and ministries.

A psychiatric evaluation for OCD is a good way to obtain necessary treatment. What should one expect in a psychiatric evaluation? This is generally done as an interview in which a patient's symptoms are identified as the chief complaint. Further clarification of these symptoms comes through discussion of their duration, how much it limits one's function, the nature of the obsessions and compulsions, recent stressors, and whether or not anything the patient has tried has been helpful. The psychiatrist will then ask for pertinent medical history such as whether or not this has occurred before and whether any particular treatments have been tried. Questions about emotional or relationship difficulties are often asked in an attempt to identify coexisting conditions or to make a more accurate alternative diagnosis. A patient's medical history including illnesses, results of recent physical evaluations, medications taken, along with relevant blood and laboratory tests are also important information to integrate into the diagnostic process. Other questions involving interpersonal relationships, drug or substance abuse, and family history of psychiatric disorders are also asked.

The psychiatrist then performs a mental status examination, which is composed of observations and questions directed at evaluating many areas of mental functioning. These include appearance, speech, mood, and cognitive abilities such as memory and concentration. Judgment and insight into the illness are also determined. Questions about suicidal, homicidal, or delusional thinking are also part of a thorough mental status examination. Given the extensive and probing questions that are explored in a psychiatric evaluation, a word must be said about confidentiality.

Professional ethics as well as common law uphold the privacy and confidentiality of all information provided by a client, patient, penitent, and so forth, to the respective professional, whether it be therapist, physician, clergyman, or attorney. Hence, unless a person gives permission, particularly in written form, information divulged in psychiatric evaluations must be kept confidential.

Discerning the difference between theological and psychological issues will lead to proper assessment of a person's difficulty. Ministers can play an important role in helping individuals afflicted with mental health problems. Christians with OCD, particularly those who suffer from excessive doubt or scrupulosity, are often anxious about their spiritual condition. They tend to focus more on God's judgment and wrath than on His grace. They tend to glean from Scripture those verses that cause them to worry about their spiritual well-being while taking only transient comfort from Scripture pertaining to God's love and forgiveness.

Ministers probably have experienced this with some members of their congregation who just cannot take comfort from the reassurances of their counsel or the promises of God. Hence, ministers educated about OCD can best identify those persons whose spiritual questioning may be a symptom of OCD or just the normal concerns of a growing believer. The differences are often subtle and elusive but are worthy of deliberation.

Anyone with OCD can be challenging to live with. Add in the kind of spiritualized scrupulosity that can accompany "faith," and any relationship can be stressed to its limits.

How People Can Help

The following are ways in which a caring person, whether it is a fellow churchgoer, family member, or a minister, can help.

1. If a person is suffering from a mental problem, make attempts to learn more about it rather than making immediate speculations or spiritual judg-

ments about his condition. There are many places where one can get information about OCD, including at the doctor's office.

2. Maintain a stance of steady encouragement. Use Scripture, but be aware that the individual will require continual reassurance and patience. It can be very frustrating trying to reassure someone who has OCD, also known as "the doubting disease." However, if you keep in mind that the doubt and anxiety represent symptoms of an illness much like a cough is a symptom of pneumonia, then you can avoid the temptation to believe that your attempts to reassure are being ignored. Instead, recall the person's usual manner of thinking prior to the development of OCD (or what we call the baseline state) as being truly representative of him.

Relationships can be stressed by an individual's bout with OCD. As a caring individual, try not to take the sufferer's idiosyncratic thoughts personally. For example, if he had contamination fears he may not enter your home or touch specific items that belong to you. Do not defend your personal cleanliness or insist that he enter your domain. However, maintain an open invitation to be in contact with you and your home because he may be able to venture out and expose himself to what he fears once he is ready. This usually occurs in the context of treatment where patients are taught coping skills and encouraged to practice exposing themselves to the object of their obsessive anxiety.

How can the minister or another caring individual

tell when someone might have OCD and be in need of professional help? If someone reveals that he is troubled by thoughts and behaviors that are described in this chapter, ask him to tell you more about these symptoms. Try to ascertain the level of distress this is causing for him and his family. Generally, most people are quite secretive about their condition, functioning quite well despite their troubling thoughts. Usually when they confide in others, their level of distress is fairly significant and the chances are good that they would benefit from professional help.

A sure sign that professional attention is necessary occurs when there is a decline in the person's ability to function at work, school, or home. Obsessive thoughts and compulsive behaviors may be so time-consuming that they prevent a person from attending to the tasks of daily living or even something as simple as getting out of the house on time. There may be a decline in the person's usual level of service or participation in the church. Activities, which previously may have been performed enthusiastically, may turn into obstacles and burdens. When questioned, the sufferer may complain that he would like to be a faithful servant but just feels so overwhelmed *all the time*. This is a good opening to provide a safe, non-judgmental opportunity to discuss his concerns.

If you discover that the person may be suffering from OCD and it is clear that functioning has been affected, professional help should be recommended. The caring individual can point out to the sufferer that treatment can preserve or restore his functioning at work, home, and church. It would also address his emotional suffering and have a positive impact on his spiritual health.

A crucial factor warranting a prompt referral to professional help is the presence of clinical depression. There is a higher risk of developing a depression in people who have obsessive-compulsive disorder. This can occur simultaneously or at different times in a person's life. The description of a clinical depression is discussed elsewhere in this book. Suffice it to say, that the presence of depression should be a signal to make a timely referral for professional help.

3. Help the individual combat the stigma that is often attached to seeking mental health services. This stigma in society regarding mental illness has crossed into many churches. Hence, sufferers with OCD symptoms are reluctant to admit their thoughts and behaviors and even much more disinclined to seek professional attention. Wise counsel from the caring individual is needed. For example, you might stress that taking care of one's mental health is akin to taking care of oneself physically and represents good stewardship of our bodies. Since this is aligned with the Lord's will for all of us, He will provide both the desire and the power to do what pleases Him.

Reassure the person that you would not think less of him if he sought help, but rather you would congratulate him for his courage. If you are ac-

quainted with any similar situations, present to the
person instances where someone has benefited
from professional help. Try to do this without providing any identifying detail about another person
as most individuals value their privacy on this
sensitive topic. Shed light on what is often an unknown. Describe what takes place in a psychiatric
examination as outlined earlier in this chapter.
Share information you have obtained on the topic
of OCD and how one finds professional help. If
you need assistance on the latter, refer to the listing of resources at the end of this book.

4. Assist the family members. Because OCD impairs
the functioning of the sufferer, it is important to
pay attention to the needs of the family and the
household. As you can imagine, OCD can plunder
the time of an entire family because of the mental
and behavioral rituals that consume the sufferer.
Job functioning may be impaired, leading to a loss
of income. Household chores may be left undone.
There is much a caring community can do to address the specific needs of the family members
until the sufferer regains his mental health. Generally speaking, many people who suffer from
OCD function despite their illness and can be re-
stored to good functioning in a timely way with
professional help and support from their friends
and families.

5. Respect the individual's confidentiality. This dic-
tum is self-explanatory. However, there may be
many areas in the course of church life where a
person's desire for privacy may be violated, inad-

vertently. For example, if a person requests prayer for the problem, it may have to be done tactfully without telling the details to those who are praying or it may have to be limited to the confines of a minister's office. One should ask permission of the sufferer should there be any reason to discuss the matter with others in the family or in the church. Many people with OCD choose to conceal their condition even when they are improving with treatment. They may be doing so for personal and valid reasons, and it would be important for the clergy and the caring individual to honor their wishes.

6. Assist the individual in getting professional help. Getting the appropriate help for the person with OCD may require some planning and research. In general, the treatment for OCD in this country involves a type of behavior therapy often in conjunction with medication. Psychologists, social workers, and Christian counselors who have specific expertise in the cognitive-behavioral or behavioral treatment of OCD are equipped to provide the talking aspect of the therapy. However, they cannot dispense medication and would have to make a referral to a psychiatrist for an appropriate medication evaluation. Sometimes, though this is not the optimal situation, such patients may go to their family doctor for medication.

A psychiatrist is a medical doctor who can conduct a psychiatric evaluation and prescribe medication appropriately. Some psychiatrists provide psychotherapy in conjunction with medication as needed and it would be advisable to see a psychiatrist in the treatment of OCD. Some hospitals in the local community may operate anxiety disorder programs, which provide multidisciplinary services for patients. They may be staffed by a combination of psychologists, social workers, counselors, and psychiatrists who offer a comprehensive treatment program. You may wish to contact your local hospital's department of psychiatry to ascertain whether or not such a program exists either at the hospital or in a community mental health clinic.

You can further inquire if there is a private psychiatrist affiliated with the hospital or in the community who has expertise in treating OCD. Your family physician may also be a source of information in providing you with a referral to a psychiatrist or therapist he believes will benefit the patient. After trying your local resources for referrals, you may wish to contact the organizations listed at the end of this book.

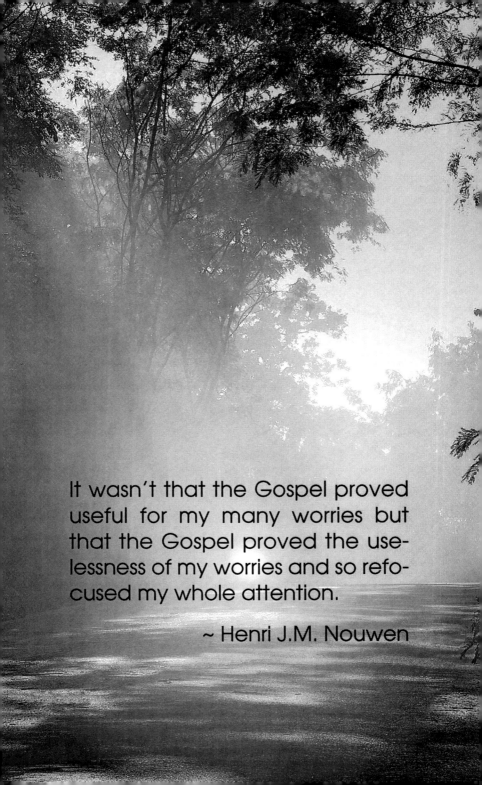

It wasn't that the Gospel proved useful for my many worries but that the Gospel proved the uselessness of my worries and so refocused my whole attention.

~ Henri J.M. Nouwen

CHAPTER 12

The Word of God

BIBLICAL PRECEPTS INTEGRATE EFFECTIVELY WITH THE TREAT-ment method called cognitive behavioral therapy (CBT).[1] Founded by Aaron T. Beck, MD, CBT refers to the parts of its name. Cognition refers to "thoughts" which the patient experiences, leading to a certain mood and ultimately a set of behaviors. These thoughts are automatic and pervasive. When a person's belief and thought are unrealistic, maladaptive, and untrue, they will behave and feel accordingly.

Anxious people often have catastrophic thoughts, directed toward the worst case scenario, which usually begins with the words "what if. . . ." This leads to fear and avoidance. The goal of CBT is to help the person monitor these misbeliefs and replace them with truth. This leads to correct behavior and prevents avoidance of activities or situations that needlessly produce fear. What better way to replace anxious thoughts than with biblical truth? CBT frees Christians to use their faith-generated principles to counter their automatic catastrophic worries. Once identified, it is affirming that such a well proven mode of treatment is so easily aligned with a biblical principle such as "we take captive every thought. . . ."[2]

Biblical teachings yield universal well-being and health, despite a stressful life. All of us struggle with many worries including concerns about our health, jobs, families, and our future. Some of these worries may represent responses to genuine stressful life situations and other worries may be due to psychological or medical conditions.

In any event, a good question is why do believers worry when Jesus, for example, tells us not to have any anxiety in anything? If worrying about the body and daily bread cannot add one iota to life, why do we do it? We know that God can adorn the lilies and feed the sparrows. Therefore, He can also attend to our personal concerns.

What are your worries both past and present? How have you coped with your fears and what role has your faith taken? As for your future concerns, God's Word can also play a role. It is a good resource to help you with anxiety. Moreover, from a therapeutic perspective, these truths should easily be integrated into the cognitive behavioral therapy (CBT) of patients who accept the truth of the Bible. In keeping with the link between Scripture and coping with anxiety using CBT, the following Bible verses and a group study tool are recommended:

> *Philippians 4:6-8*
> *Do not be anxious about anything, but in every situation, by prayer and petition, with thanksgiving, present your requests to God. And the peace of God, which transcends all understanding, will guard your hearts and your minds in Christ Jesus. Finally, brothers and sisters, whatever is true, whatever is noble, whatever is right, whatever is pure, whatever is lovely, whatever is admirable . . . think about such things.*

This is one of the most popular passages in Scripture addressing anxiety and for good reason. It provides a series of steps to take when one is anxious:

1. Halt the anxious thinking.
2. Turn your attention to God.
3. Pray to Him regarding the stressor.
4. Thank Him for what you are thankful for.
5. Having given Him your anxious thoughts, turn your mind to that which is noble, pure, lovely, and admirable.
6. Regarding what is lovely, visualize the beautiful scenes in nature that you have witnessed and find calming.
7. Practice the above steps.

It is beneficial to meditate on the truth of these verses. If you take the steps derived from the passage you will influence the mental processes generating anxiety. This is biblically directed cognitive restructuring at its finest.

> *Isaiah 41:10*
> *So do not fear, for I am with you; do not be dismayed, for I am your God. I will strengthen you and help you; I will uphold you with my righteous right hand.*

The promise of God's strength, assistance and support along the turbulent road of life is reason to remain calm and unperplexed. People do well in hard times, and may even thrive, when there is adequate support. But when that help comes from an Almighty source, there is greater reason for tranquility instead of fear.

Proverbs 1:33
. . . but whoever listens to me [Wisdom] will live in
safety and be at ease, without fear of harm.

Proverbial wisdom, as described here, is God's instruction. It provides a foundation as well as guidelines for being at ease and safe. Despite any onslaught of real life stressors or emotional turbulence caused by anxious thinking, the essential truth for the believing Christian is that there is "no fear of harm."

Psalm 23:4
Even though I walk through the darkest valley, I will
fear no evil, for you are with me; your rod and your
staff, they comfort me.

Many patients with anxiety disorders have an overwhelming fear and preoccupation with having or developing a serious medical illness such as cancer or a heart attack, because the end result is death. One does not need to have an anxiety disorder in order to fear death. In our strongly thanatophobic (death-fearing) society, death is a force to be conquered, grieved, processed, denied, avoided, and if all else fails, delayed. Religious faith offers another solution. This Scripture verse, spoken at many funerals, indicates that death or "walking through the valley of the shadow of death" need not to be feared in the presence of a God who comforts. Death can bring on sadness and a sense of loss or separation, but it does not need to be feared. The strength of this concept lies in the person's ability to incorporate it into his belief system. While it may be futile to insist that a person accept this belief while in the throes of a panic attack, this idea can be comprehended at the appropriate time. Simply observe its usefulness during funeral services. Many times, the verse is also uttered in prayer during a time of imminent peril, the "foxhole" experiences of a person's life.

Psalm 37:23
The Lord makes firm the steps of the one who delights in him. . . .

An enormous amount of stress is generated by doing what is illegal, immoral, or just plain wrong. In contrast, if one stays within the confines of moral or civil law and similarly if a Christian walks in a path consistent with God's way, he does not bring upon himself the stress and anxiety that accompanies wrongdoing. In fact, the Lord makes his "steps firm." This can be an important principle of stress management and prevention.

Even in this age of anxiety, we can have "no worries," because God is with us at all times and in every circumstance that might cause even the most courageous to be afraid.

Mark 6:45-51
Immediately Jesus made his disciples get into the boat and go on ahead of him to Bethsaida, while he dismissed the crowd. After leaving them, he went up on a mountainside to pray. Later that night, the boat was in the middle of the lake, and he was alone on land. He saw the disciples straining at the oars, because the wind was against them. Shortly before dawn he went out to them, walking on the lake. He was about to pass by them, but when they saw him walking on the lake, they thought he was a ghost. They cried out, because they all saw him and were terrified. Immediately he spoke to them and said,

"Take courage! It is I. Don't be afraid." Then he climbed into the boat with them, and the wind died down. They were completely amazed. . . .

The Bible offers us many snapshots of human fear and anxiety and God's response to them. Jesus' reassurance to the disciples in the midst of rough water is, "Take courage! It is I." Jesus being powerfully God yet empathetically human is a source of true comfort and amazement to his frightened disciples. This image is by no means lost on today's Christians.

In the practical application of this image to the worrying Christian today, consider the use of "visualization techniques" as part of relaxation exercises. These techniques involve having the person mentally visualize a calming, restful scene of his or her own choice. Common examples would be a sunny beach scene, a warm meadow on a spring day, or a gentle waterfall, which are generally chosen from the individual's personal repertoire of experiences. Christians can and often do choose scenes from a biblical passage that convey to them a sense of calm. The picture of Jesus' strong and comforting presence as portrayed in this passage can be utilized in visualization techniques to enhance relaxation. Another biblical image involves picturing oneself as a tree planted by a stream of water which is a metaphor for a person who delights and meditates on God's Word. Calming biblical images are highly individualized and should be derived from one's personal experience. Once identified, they can be incorporated into that person's program of relaxation.

Psalm 112:1-9
Praise the LORD.
Blessed are those who fear the LORD,
who find great delight in his commands.
Their children will be mighty in the land;
the generation of the upright will be blessed.

Wealth and riches are in their houses,
*   and their righteousness endures forever.*
Even in darkness light dawns for the upright,
*   for those who are gracious and compassionate*
*   and righteous.*
Good will come to those who are generous and
*   lend freely,*
*   who conduct their affairs with justice.*
Surely the righteous will never be shaken;
*   they will be remembered forever.*
They will have no fear of bad news;
*   their hearts are steadfast, trusting in the LORD.*
Their hearts are secure, they will have no fear;
*   in the end they will look in triumph on their foes.*
They have freely scattered their gifts to the poor,
*   their righteousness endures forever;*
*   their horn will be lifted high in honor. . . .*

Holy fear results in no fear. That is the essence of this passage from the psalmist. The blessings that ensue from fearing the Lord are manifold. They comprise the areas of life that worry many people today—children, wealth, time, security, and honor. Reverential fear of the Lord, combined with obedience to God's commands, and personal compassion and generosity form the basis for a sanctified life.

> *John 16:33*
> *I have told you these things, so that in me you may*
> *have peace. In this world you will have trouble. But*
> *take heart! I have overcome the world.*

This verse is Jesus' promise to his disciples. His realistic foretelling of the troubles that the world will bring is countered by the assurance that He has guaranteed their peace. In the same way, Christians need to understand that although they will experience stresses in their lives, they can turn their thoughts to God who has overcome the world and maintain inner tranquility. Even more important is this message for the person prone to anxiety who generally appraises every situation, good or bad, as having potential for catastrophe. He or she should employ this biblical truth to restructure his or her automatic, negativistic, anxiety-provoking thoughts to those which are more realistic, positive, and pacifying.

> *Romans 8:15-16*
> *The Spirit you received does not make you slaves, so that you live in fear again; rather, the Spirit you received brought about your adoption to sonship. And by him we cry, "Abba, Father." The Spirit himself testifies with our spirit that we are God's children.*

Believing that we are children of God through Christ rather than slaves to sin is the crux of the Christian faith. "Abba" is like the word "Daddy" that many very young children utter as one of their first words. We can expect to master fear because of the special standing of sonship to Abba, (our dear) Father. Our thoughts should be conformed to this new relationship. Hence, anxious people need to focus on God's parental love and not the judgment of a harsh slave driver.

> *2 Thessalonians 3:3*
> *But the Lord is faithful, and he will strengthen you and protect you from the evil one.*

The doctrine of the devil or the "evil one" is totally in the theological realm and has no real counterpart in the psychological world. Granted, there are attempts at psychological explanations for the entity of the devil or evil such as delusions but as a real concrete person, only fundamental Christian faith provides for its definition. Given that Christians believe in satanic oppression as one cause of stress and anxiety, it would be pragmatic and even therapeutic to offer biblical reassurance of protection from the evil one. For many Christians, knowing that the devil may be behind much of their fear and anxiety gives them enough impetus to persevere and function despite great fear or obstacle. Somehow the very realization that they are experiencing fear and affliction by the evil one because they are on the right track of living a holy life renders some Christians ready to join battle in a spiritual sense. Furthermore when there is biblical support for God's power and might over the evil one and His ability to protect, many Christians take great comfort even while struggling. This doctrine remains a theologically based tool which plays a vital role in the church's work against anxiety.

> When fears assail, believers have two advantages: What they know—God loves them and has in His mind only their best; and, Who they know— a God Who always keeps His promises.

> *Hebrews 13:6*
> *So we say with confidence. "The Lord is my helper;*
> *I will not be afraid. What can mere mortals do to*
> *me?"*

When anxious patients speak of the dread they anticipate in a given situation, I often ask them, "Tell me, what do you think is the worst that can happen?" When they actually go through the process, they realize that the worst is really not so bad. It certainly does not merit the kind of fear they were experiencing. The rhetorical query, "What can mere mortals do to me?" is analogous to my line of questioning. And more importantly, because Christians have the advantage of knowing that the Lord is their helper in any situation that could happen, they can choose not to fear.

Psalm 27:1-14
The LORD is my light and my salvation—
  whom shall I fear?
The LORD is the stronghold of my life—
  of whom shall I be afraid?
When the wicked advance against me
  to devour me,
it is my enemies and my foes
  who will stumble and fall.
Though an army besiege me,
  my heart will not fear;
though war break out against me,
  even then I will be confident.
One thing I ask from the LORD,
  this only do I seek:
that I may dwell in the house of the LORD
  all the days of my life,
to gaze on the beauty of the LORD
  and to seek him in his temple.
For in the day of trouble
  he will keep me safe in his dwelling;
he will hide me in the shelter of his sacred tent
  and set me high upon a rock.
Then my head will be exalted
  above the enemies who surround me;
at his sacred tent I will sacrifice with shouts of joy;
  I will sing and make music to the LORD.
Hear my voice when I call, LORD;

be merciful to me and answer me.
My heart says of you, "Seek his face!"
Your face, LORD, I will seek.
Do not hide your face from me,
do not turn your servant away in anger;
you have been my helper.
Do not reject me or forsake me,
God my Savior.
Though my father and mother forsake me,
the LORD will receive me.
Teach me your way, LORD;
lead me in a straight path
because of my oppressors.
Do not turn me over to the desire of my foes,
for false witnesses rise up against me,
spouting malicious accusations.
I remain confident of this:
I will see the goodness of the LORD
in the land of the living.
Wait for the LORD;
be strong and take heart
and wait for the LORD.

This prayer juxtaposes two combating themes. One is modified by words such as "light," "salvation," "stronghold," "confident," "joy," "make music," "goodness," "take heart," and "wait for the Lord." Opposing thoughts are expressed in the words "fear," "stumble," "war," "enemies," and "oppressors."

This prayer expresses the cognitive struggle of a man trying to use his thoughts to reduce the anxiety generated by a forceful onslaught of fear-producing images. This anxiety is most likely situationally induced. The cognitive battle and its success is based on the belief in the sovereignty of God. This prayer illustrates the cognitive processes of many Christians undergoing stress. For many, it represents a powerful, theologically generated coping skill.

> *Psalm 56:3-4*
> *When I am afraid, I put my trust in you. In God,*
> *whose word I praise—in God I trust and am not*
> *afraid. What can mere mortals do to me?*

The sequence of thoughts in this passage is signaled by the emotion of fear. The response of the believer is to confront fear by affirming trust in God and His word. This acknowledgement results in the shift to the new state, "I will not be afraid." This is the essence of Christian cognitive restructuring, that is, the change in mood rendered by adopting into one's cognition, realities—in this case spiritual—for the purpose of altering the mood state. Once the quelling of the fear is achieved, it is further bolstered by the rhetorical question, "What can mere mortals do to me?" For the believer, this reflection underscores the notion that there is nothing that mortal man can inflict upon the believer that is beyond the scope of God's trustworthy care and protection.

> Anyone can change their mood by changing their thoughts. Believers can *exchange* their fears for faith by personalizing the fact that God is for them.

> *Proverbs 12:25*
> *Anxiety weighs down the heart,*
> *but a kind word cheers it up.*

When caring for the anxious sufferers in your church, do not underestimate the power of an encouraging word. Even if the comfort is temporary, it provides a moment of relief by cheering the heart. This is supported by biblical wisdom and can be done quite well by anybody who is willing.

> *Jeremiah 29:11-13*
> *"For I know the plans I have for you," declares the Lord, "plans to prosper you and not to harm you, plans to give you hope and a future. Then you will call on me and come and pray to me, and I will listen to you. You will seek me and find me when you seek me with all your heart."*

The future is often plagued with misgivings and worry for anxious people. Circumstantial changes are often unsettling and anxiety-provoking. This verse indicates that one can counter worries about potential problems by acknowledging, in faith, that God has plans to prosper and not to harm. One can forbear changes and crises by keeping a positive focus on the future based on this verse.

> *Matthew 10:29-31*
> *Are not two sparrows sold for a penny? Yet not one of them will fall to the ground outside your Father's care. And even the very hairs of your head are all numbered. So don't be afraid; you are worth more than many sparrows.*

The anxious Christian needs to know that God is in control even though he feels out of control as a result of worry. He also needs to understand his great personal worth to a God who will care for him. Understanding these biblical precepts will offset the concerns that plague him and temper the emotion of anxiety.

Matthew 14:22-27
Immediately Jesus made the disciples get into the
boat and go on ahead of him to the other side, while
he dismissed the crowd. After he had dismissed
them, he went up on a mountainside by himself to
pray. Later that night, he was there alone, and the
boat was already a considerable distance from land,
buffeted by the waves because the wind was against
it. Shortly before dawn Jesus went out to them,
walking on the lake. When the disciples saw him
walking on the lake, they were terrified. "It's a
ghost," they said, and cried out in fear. But Jesus
immediately said to them: "Take courage! It is I.
Don't be afraid."

The disciples were afraid when they saw Jesus walking on the water toward them and concluded, "It's a ghost." Their fear, understandingly, heightened by the buffeting waves, was in response to a misperception. This was not a ghost but their friend and teacher. Anxiety often occurs in response to misperceptions and therefore it is always important to evaluate any situation carefully before making anxiety provoking conclusions.

2 Corinthians 1:3-4
Praise be to the God and Father of our Lord Jesus
Christ, the Father of compassion and the God of all
comfort, who comforts us in all our troubles, so that
we can comfort those in any trouble with the com-
fort we ourselves receive from God.

The comforting nature of God is the foundation for the comfort that Christians give to each other. Because He has comforted them in their own individual difficulties, they are enabled to help others in any trouble with the same kind of divinely originated comfort they have received. This kind of comfort is far more valuable than any charitable activity of purely human origin. Though such endeavors are good in themselves, the comfort that can be offered by believers has eternal value since it is linked to the eternal God, from Whom it flowed in the first place.

> *2 Timothy 1:7*
> *For the Spirit God gave us does not make us timid,*
> *but gives us power, love and self-discipline.*

In working with phobic patients, I have recognized that those who succeed in mastering their fears have two main strengths. One is a strong motivation and the other is the self-discipline and perseverance it takes to endure anxious moments in order to overcome the anxiety previously connected to a feared stimulus. We are given power, love, and self-discipline which can be employed along with some professional counseling to overcome anxiety.

> *1 Chronicles 28:20*
> *David also said to Solomon his son, "Be strong and*
> *courageous, and do the work. Do not be afraid or*
> *discouraged, for the Lord God, my God, is with you.*
> *He will not fail you or forsake you until all the work*
> *for the service of the temple of the Lord is finished."*

When we are called by God to perform a task, often there are difficult challenges in the process of completing it. Facing our fears is no easy feat and may lead some to give up, resulting in feelings of defeat and regret. This promise, for those who believe it, provides the cognitive impetus to persevere.

> *Lamentations 3:22-23*
> *Because of the Lord's great love we are not consumed, for his compassions never fail.*

They are new every morning; great is your faith-fulness.

People speak in terms of being "consumed" with worry, anxiety, or doubt. Obsessions can be viewed as a form of mental consumption. And despite the power of strong human emotion, Christians are anchored by this promise: they are not consumed. That is, though they feel embattled, they are not crushed; though they feel drained, they are not exhausted. The renewal of God's compassion is a source of new hope each morning and provides faithful reassurance despite difficult times.

> *Hebrews 4:14-16*
> *Therefore, since we have a great high priest who has ascended into heaven, Jesus the Son of God, let us hold firmly to the faith we profess. For we do not have a high priest who is unable to empathize with our weaknesses, but we have one who has been tempted in every way, just as we are.... Let us then approach God's throne of grace with confidence, so that we may receive mercy and find grace to help us in our time of need.*

Having a merciful and sympathetic "high priest," who can empathize with our anxiety provides us with the confidence to persevere. It is much like having a "listening ear" who is also a strong advocate and source of help. Because of this, anxious Christians do not have to live in self-condemnation for their anxiety. They only need to focus their efforts on overcoming it.

> *2 Corinthians 7:5-7*
> *For when we came into Macedonia, we had no rest, but we were harassed at every turn—conflicts on the outside, fears within. But God, who comforts the*

downcast, comforted us by the coming of Titus, and not only by his coming but also by the comfort you had given him. He told us about your longing for me, your deep sorrow, your ardent concern for me, so that my joy was greater than ever.

The therapeutic value of Christian caring and concern is one of the major contributions of the church. Paul, at this point in his ministry, would be a good candidate for modern day stress management seminars. His body had no rest; he was struggling with external conflicts, and experiencing internal fears. He describes the tremendous comfort and relief at the appearance of a fellow colleague, Titus. Moreover, Paul spoke of the joy he derived from hearing about the Corinthian's sympathy, burden, and care for him. This supportive role is what the ideal church has done well throughout the centuries.

One reason we find so much help and hope in the Scriptures is that in its pages we often see characters facing situations a lot like those we face on a daily basis.

Proverbs 3:25-26
Have no fear of sudden disaster or of the ruin that overtakes the wicked, for the Lord will be at your side and will keep your foot from being snared.

The unpredictability and damaging consequences of sudden disaster frighten many. People take multiple precautions for all kinds of catastrophe, but there is no real guarantee that the measures they take will work. One need not live in fear of sudden disaster. That sort of life is emotionally crippling and unnecessary. For Christians, this verse reminds them of the security they have in God.

> *Isaiah 26:3*
> *The steadfast of mind You will keep in perfect peace,*
> *because he trusts in You (NASB).*

This is one author's favorite verse as it highlights the importance of training one's mind to be steadfast on the Lord. Trusting in God will enable one to have "perfect peace," even in times that might otherwise cause stress and anxiety.

> *Luke 2:10-11*
> *But the angel said to them, "Do not be afraid. I bring you good news that will cause great joy for all the people. Today in the town of David a Savior has been born to you; he is the Messiah, the Lord."*

"Fear not" is the good news Christians can trust!

> *John 14:27*
> *Peace I leave with you; my peace I give you. I do not give to you as the world gives. Do not let your hearts be troubled and do not be afraid.*

In Jesus' final instructions to His closest friends, the disciples, He speaks of a transcendent peace that only can come from Him, a divine source. The promise of favor, forgiveness, and eternal life infinitely extends the coping armamentarium available to Christians.

Practical Application of these Principles

The following is a tool that can be used in a group setting in a church or community of faith. It is written in the form of a Bible study. Participants in such a group may find that as they answer the questions together the process allows them to confront some of their worries. Therapeutic benefits such as emotional support, bonding, dispelling of isolation, and sharing of coping resources will occur.

Bible Study on Anxiety

John 16:33
Are stressful conditions part of a Christian's life?

Mark 6:45-51
What is Jesus' attitude toward Christians who are afraid?

Proverbs 1:33
How can you live at ease and safety?

Philippians 4:6-9
What steps should you take when you are anxious? What is the hardest step for you?

Psalm 56:3-4
How does one confront fear?

Proverbs 12:25
How can you help an anxious person?

Luke 10: 38-42
When was the last time you were "worried and upset?"

2 Corinthians 7:5-7
Who did God use to comfort Paul in his stress? Did God use anyone to comfort you? Who? How?

Jeremiah 29:11-13
What does God say to the Christian who is anxious about the future?

Luke 2:10-11
Explain the essential truth that permits one to "Fear not!"

Resources

American Psychiatric Association
1000 Wilson Boulevard, Suite 1825
Arlington, VA, 22209
Telephone: 888-35-PSYCH (888-357-7924)
Web-page: www.psychiatry.org
E-mail: apa@psych.org

American Psychological Association
750 First Street NE
Washington, DC, 20002-4242
Telephone: 800-374-2721
Web-page: www.apa.org

Anxiety and Depression Association of America
8701 Georgia Ave., #412
Silver Spring, MD, 20910
Telephone: 240-485-1001
Web-page: www.adaa.org

Association for Behavioral and Cognitive Therapies
305 7th Ave., 16th Floor
New York, NY, 10001
Telephone: 212-647-1890
Web-page: www.abct.org

Body and Soul Fitness
PO Box 2288
Germantown, MD, 20875-2288
Telephone: 888-660-7685 / 301-258-1018
Web-page: www.bodyandsoul.org
E-mail: info@bodyandsoul.org

Depression and Bipolar Support Alliance
730 North Franklin Street, Suite 501
Chicago, IL, 60654-7225
Telephone: 800-826-3632
Web-page: www.dbsalliance.org

Focus On the Family Program
Focus on the Family
8605 Explorer Drive
Colorado Springs, CO, 80920-1051
Telephone: 800-A-FAMILY (800-232-6459)
Monday–Friday, 6:00am–8:00pm, Mountain Time
Web-page: www.foccusonthefamily.com
E-mail: help@FocusOnTheFamily.com

Link Care Center
1734 West Shaw Avenue
Fresno, CA, 93711
Telephone: 559-439-5920
Web-page: www.linkcare.org

National Domestic Violence Hotline
Telephone: 1-800-799-SAFE (800-799-7233)
Web-page: www.thehotline.org

National Institute of Mental Health
National Institute of Mental Health
Science Writing, Press, and Dissemination Branch
6001 Executive Blvd., Room 6200, MSC 9663
Bethesda, MD, 20892-9663
Telephone: 301-443-4513
Web-page: www.nimh.nih.gov
Live help online chat Monday–Friday, 8:30am–5:00pm ET

North American Society for Psychosocial Obstetrics and Gynecology (NASPOG)
NASPOG National Office
8213 Lakenheath Way
Potomac, MD, 20854
Telephone: 301-983-6282
Web-page: www.naspog.org
E-mail: info@naspog.org

Pacific Garden Mission
1458 South Canal Street
Chicago, Illinois, 60607
Telephone: 312-492-9410
Web-page: www.pgm.org
E-mail: welchs@pgm.org

Postpartum Support International
Local help listed under webpage
Telephone: 800-944-4PPD (800-944-4773)
Web-page: www.postpartum.net

Endnotes

Chapter 2
Panic – "The Oppressor"

1. J. Rosenbaum, "Treatment of Panic Disorder: The State of Art," *Journal of Clinical Psychiatry* 58, no. 2 (1997): 3.
2. American Psychiatric Association, *The Diagnostic and Statistical Manual of Mental Disorders*, 5th Edition (Arlington, VA: American Psychiatric Publishing, 2013), 230.
3. Ibid., 226.
4. Ibid., 228.

Chapter 3
A Treatment Described

1. Edmund Jacobson, *Progressive Relaxation: A Physiological and Clinical Investigation of Muscular States and Their Significance in Psychology and Medical Practice* (Chicago: University of Chicago Press, 1938).

Chapter 5
Generalized Anxiety Disorder – "The Individual and the Church"

1. American Psychiatric Association, *The Diagnostic and Statistical Manual of Mental Disorders*, 5th Edition (Arlington, VA: American Psychiatric Publishing, 2013), 222.

Chapter 6
Phobias

1. American Psychiatric Association, *The Diagnostic and Statistical Manual of Mental Disorders*, 5th Edition (Arlington, VA: American Psychiatric Publishing, 2013), 197-198.

Chapter 7
Agoraphobia

1. American Psychiatric Association, *The Diagnostic and Statistical Manual of Mental Disorders*, 5th Edition (Arlington, VA: American Psychiatric Publishing, 2013), 217.

Chapter 8
Post-Traumatic Stress Disorder – A Specific Case

1. American Psychiatric Association, *The Diagnostic and Statistical Manual of Mental Disorders*, 5th Edition (Arlington, VA: American Psychiatric Publishing, 2013), 271-272.

Chapter 9
Depression – "An Illness, Not A Weakness"

1. NIMH, "NIMH – Statistics – Major Depression Among Adults"
    NIMH.NIH.gov, (accessed July 13, 2014),
    http://www.nimh.nih.gov/statistics/1MDD_ADULT.shtml.
2. American Psychiatric Association, *The Diagnostic and Statistical Manual of Mental Disorders*, 5th Edition (Arlington, VA: American Psychiatric Publishing, 2013), 160-161.
3. Quote from American Psychiatric Association's literature for National Depression Screening Day.
4. American Psychiatric Association, *The Diagnostic and Statistical Manual of Mental Disorders*, 5th Edition (Arlington, VA: American Psychiatric Publishing, 2013), 186-187.
5. Ibid.

Chapter 10
Premenstrual Dysphoric Disorder

1. American Psychiatric Association, *The Diagnostic and Statistical Manual of Mental Disorders*, 5th Edition (Arlington, VA: American Psychiatric Publishing, 2013), 171-172.
2. Mary Jane Minkin, *What Every Woman Should Know About Menopause* (New Haven, Connecticut: Yale University Press, 1996), 38-39.
3. K. Yonkers, U. Halgreich, E. Freeman, C. Brown, J. Endicott, E. Frank, B. Parry, T. Pearlstein, S. Severino, A. Stout, S. Stone, W. Harrison, "Symptomatic Improvement of Premenstrual Dysphoria With Sertraline Treatment: A Randomized Control Trial," *Journal of American Medical Association*, no. 278(12) (September 24, 1997): 983-988.

Chapter 11
Obsessions and Compulsions

1. American Psychiatric Association, *The Diagnostic and Statistical Manual of Mental Disorders*, 5th Edition (Arlington, VA: American Psychiatric Publishing, 2013), 237.
2. Personal communication from Dr. Bruce Ballard, Associate Dean of Medical Students at Cornell University Medical College.

Chapter 12
The Word of God

1. Aaron T. Beck, Gary Emery, and Ruth Greenberg, *Anxiety Disorders and Phobias: A Cognitive Perspective* (New York: Basic Books, 1985).

Bibliography

American Psychiatric Association, *The Diagnostic and Statistical Manual of Mental Disorders, 5th Edition*, Virginia: American Psychiatric Publishing, 2013.

Beck, Aaron T., Emery, Gary, and Greenberg, Ruth, *Anxiety Disorders and Phobias: A Cognitive Perspective*, New York: Basic Books, 1985.

Jacobson, Edmund. *Progressive Relaxation: A Physiological and Clinical Investigation of Muscular States and Their Significance in Psychology and Medical Practice*, Chicago: University of Chicago Press, 1938.

Minkin, Mary Jane. *What Every Woman Should Know About Menopause*, Connecticut: Yale University Press, 1996.

"NIMH – Statistics – Major Depression Among Adults." *National Institute of Mental Health.* Accessed July 13, 2014. *http://www.nimh.nih.gov/statistics/1MDD_ADULT.shtml.*

Rosenbaum, Jerrold. "Treatment of Panic Disorder: The State of Art." *Journal of Clinical Psychiatry* 58, no. 2 (1997): 3.

Yonkers, KA., Halgreich, U., Freeman, E., Brown, C., Endicott, J., Frank, E., Parry, B., Pearlstein, T., Severino, S., Stout, A., Harrison, W., "Symptomatic Improvement of Premenstrual Dysphoria with Sertraline Treatment: A Randomized Control Trial," *Journal of American Medical Association*, no. 278(12), (1997): 983-988.

About the Author

Dr. Elaine Leong Eng, a Distinguished Fellow of the American Psychiatric Association, is a graduate of Princeton University and the Albert Einstein College of Medicine. She is Clinical Assistant Professor of Psychiatry in the Department of Obstetrics and Gynecology at Weill-Cornell Medical College and Associate Professor of Mental Health Counseling at Nyack College's Alliance Graduate School of Counseling and Alliance Theological Seminary. Dr. Eng integrates faith, medicine, and psychological knowledge to provide mental health education to many audiences. Avenues for this include international and domestic speaking and writing. Her other books include *The Transforming Power of Story: How Telling Your Story Brings Hope to Others and Healing to Yourself*. She serves with the Christian Medical and Dental Associations to bring psychiatric updates and counseling to those serving abroad. Awards given to her include the Dr. Paul Kay Award for her writing, the Queen's County Psychiatric Society's award for "outstanding inspirational leadership," and Heartbeat International's Servant Leadership Award. She is married, the mother of two grown children, and owner of a beautiful Labrador retriever.

Resources from Healthy Life Press

Unless otherwise noted on the site itself, shipping is free for all products purchased through *www.healthylifepress.com.*

New Releases - Fall 2014

Mommy, What's 'Died' Mean? - How the Butterfly Story Helped Little Dave Understand His Grandpa's Death, by Linda Swain Gill; Illustrated by David Lee Bass (a.k.a. "Little Dave") – Designed to assist Christian parents and other adults who love and care about children to talk with them about the difficult subject of death, the story traces a small child's experience following his grandpa's and shows how his mother sensitively answered his questions about death by using simple examples derived from the birth of a butterfly. Little Dave's story is colorfully illustrated and designed for a child and parent or trusted adult to read together. The story has been created especially for children from pre-kindergarten through 4th grade. Discussion questions are included for each story page to help determine how much the child understands. A simple imitation game is also included to help involve the child in the story. Several pages at the end of the book contain suggestions about how to discuss death and dying with children of various ages. (**Full-color printed book:** $14.99; PDF eBook: $9.99; both together: $19.99 – direct from publisher; printed books and eBooks available at *www.Amazon.com*; *www.BN.com*; *www.deepershopping.com*, and wherever books are sold.)

No Worries - Spiritual and Mental Health Counseling for Anxiety, by Elaine Leong Eng, MD – Offering a unique spiritual and mental health perspective on a major malady of our age, this practicing Christian psychiatrist has packed a dose of reality mixed with medicine and faith into a book aimed at informing, inspiring, and equipping those who wish to better help those who struggle with anxiety and related disorders, both inside  and outside the church. As one endorser said, "I travel all over the world. I see fellow believers suffering from different forms of anxiety and worry. Dr. Eng's book gives me tools to recognize when people are suffering and how to encourage them to get the help they need." (Printed book: $19.99; PDF eBook: $9.99; both together: $24.99 – direct from publisher; printed books and eBooks available at *www.Amazon.com*; *www.BN.com*; *www.deepershopping.com*, and wherever books are sold.)

If God Is So Good, Why Do I Hurt So Bad?, by David B. Biebel, DMin – This **25th Anniversary Edition** of a best-selling classic (over 200,000 copies in print worldwide, in a dozen languages) is the book's first major revision since its initial release in 1989. This new version features additional original material related to the conundrum of suffering and faith (with principles learned along the way), and chapter ending questions for personal or group use. Endorser Sheila Walsh wrote, "I believe this is one of the most profound, empathetic and beautiful books ever written on the subject of suffering and loss. There is no attempt to quickly ease our pain but rather, with an understanding born in the crucible God uniquely designed for him, David offers a place to stand, a place to fall and a place to rise again. This book left an indelible mark on my heart over twenty years ago and now with this new release the gift is fresh and fragrant. I highly commend this to you!" (Printed book: $14.99; PDF eBook: $9.99; both together: $19.95 – direct from publisher; printed books and eBooks available at *www.Amazon.com*; *www.BN.com*; *www.deepershopping.com*, and wherever books are sold.)

EARLIER RELEASES

We've Got Mail: The New Testament Letters in Modern English – As Relevant Today as Ever! by Rev. Warren C. Biebel, Jr. – A modern English paraphrase of the New Testament Letters, sure to inspire in readers a loving appreciation for God's Word. (Printed book: $9.95; PDF eBook: $6.95; both together: $15.00 – direct from publisher; printed books and eBooks available at *www.Amazon.com*; *www.BN.com*; *www.deepershopping.com*, and wherever books are sold.)

Hearth & Home – Recipes for Life, by Karey Swan (7th Edition) – Far more than a cookbook, this classic is a life book, with recipes for life as well as for great food. Karey describes how to buy and prepare from scratch a wide variety of tantalizing dishes, while weaving into the book's fabric the wisdom of the ages plus the recipe that she and her husband used to raise their kids. A great gift for Christmas or for a new bride. (Perfect Bound book [8 x 10, glossy cover]: $17.95; PDF eBook: $12.95; both together: $24.95 – direct from publisher; printed books and eBooks available at *www.Amazon.com*; *www.BN.com*; *www.deepershopping.com*, and wherever books are sold.)

Who Me, Pray? Prayer 101: Praying Aloud, for Beginners, by Gary A. Burlingame – Who Me, Pray? is a practical guide for prayer, based on Jesus' direction in "The Lord's Prayer," with examples provided for use in typical situations where you might be asked or expected to pray in public. (Printed book: $6.95; PDF eBook: $2.99; both together: $7.95 – direct from publisher; printed books and eBooks available at *www.Amazon.com*; *www.BN. com*; *www.deepershopping.com*, and wherever books are sold.)

My Broken Heart Sings, the poetry of Gary Burlingame – In 1987, Gary and his wife Debbie lost their son Christopher John, at only six months of age, to a chronic lung disease. This life-changing experience gave them a special heart for helping others through similar loss and pain. (Printed book: $10.95; PDF eBook: $6.95; both together: $13.95 – direct from publisher; printed books and eBooks available at *www.Amazon.com*; *www. BN.com*; *www.deepershopping.com*, and wherever books are sold.)

After Normal: One Teen's Journey Following Her Brother's Death, by Diane Aggen – Based on a journal the author kept following her younger brother's death. It offers helpful insights and understanding for teens facing a similar loss or for those who might wish to understand and help teens facing a similar loss. (Printed book: $11.95; PDF eBook: $6.95; both together: $15.00 – direct from publisher; printed books and eBooks available at *www.Amazon.com*; *www.BN.com*; *www.deepershopping.com*, and wherever books are sold.)

In the Unlikely Event of a Water Landing – Lessons Learned from Landing in the Hudson River, by Andrew Jamison, MD – The author was flying standby on US Airways Flight 1549 toward Charlotte on January 15, 2009, from New York City, where he had been interviewing for a residency position. Little did he know that the next stop would be the Hudson River. Riveting and inspirational, this book would be especially helpful for people in need of hope and encouragement. (Printed book: $8.95; PDF eBook: $6.95; both together: $12.95 – direct from publisher; printed books and eBooks available at *www.Amazon.com*; *www.BN.com*; *www.deepershopping.com*, and wherever books are sold.)

Finding Martians in the Dark – Everything I Needed to Know About Teaching Took Me Only 30 Years to Learn, by Dan M. Biebel – Packed with wise advice based on hard experience, and laced with humor, this book is a perfect teacher's gift year-round. Susan J. Wegmann, PhD, says, "Biebel's sardonic wit is mellowed by a genuine love for kids and teaching. . . . A Whitman-like sensibility flows through his stories of teaching, learning, and life." (Printed book: $10.95; PDF eBook: $6.95; Together: $15.00 – direct from publisher; printed books and eBooks available at *www.Amazon.com*; *www.BN.com*; *www.deepershopping.com*, and wherever books are sold.)

Because We're Family and **Because We're Friends**, by Gary A. Burlingame – Sometimes things related to faith can be hard to discuss with your family and friends. These booklets are designed to be given as gifts, to help you open the door to discussing spiritual matters with family members and friends who are open to such a conversation. (Printed book: $5.95 each; PDF eBook: $4.95 each; both together: $9.95 [printed & eBook of the same title] – direct from publisher; printed books and eBooks available at *www.Amazon.com*; *www.BN.com*; *www.deepershopping.com*, and wherever books are sold.)

The Transforming Power of Story: How Telling Your Story Brings Hope to Others and Healing to Yourself, by Elaine Leong Eng, MD, and David B. Biebel, DMin – This book demonstrates, through multiple true life stories, how sharing one's story, especially in a group setting, can bring hope to listeners and healing to the one who shares. Individuals facing difficulties will find this book greatly encouraging. (Printed book: $14.99; PDF eBook: $9.99; both together: $19.99 – direct from publisher; printed books and eBooks available at *www.Amazon.com*; *www.BN.com*; *www.deepershopping.com*, and wherever books are sold.)

You Deserved a Better Father: Good Parenting Takes a Plan, by Robb Brandt, MD – About parenting by intention, and other lessons the author learned through the loss of his firstborn son. It is especially for parents who believe that bits and pieces of leftover time will be enough for their own children. (Printed book: $12.95 each; PDF eBook: $6.95; both together: $17.95 – direct from publisher; printed books and eBooks available at

www.Amazon.com; *www.BN.com*; *www.deepershopping.com*, and wherever books are sold.)

eBook Cover

Printed Cover

Jonathan, You Left Too Soon, by David B. Biebel, DMin – One pastor's journey through the loss of his son, into the darkness of depression, and back into the light of joy again, emerging with a renewed sense of mission. (Printed book: $12.95; PDF eBook: $5.99; both together: $15.00 – direct from publisher; printed books and eBooks available at *www.Amazon.com*; *www.BN.com*; *www.deepershopping. com*, and wherever books are sold.)

Unless otherwise noted on the site itself, shipping is free for all products purchased through www.healthylifepress.com.

The Spiritual Fitness Checkup for the 50-Something Woman, by Sharon V. King, PhD – Following the stages of a routine medical exam, the author describes ten spiritual fitness "checkups" midlife women can conduct to assess their spiritual health and tone up their relationship with God. Each checkup consists of the author's personal reflections, a Scripture reference for meditation, and a "Spiritual Pulse Check," with exercises readers can use for personal application. (Printed book: $8.95; PDF eBook: $6.95; both together: $12.95 – direct from publisher; printed books and eBooks available at *www.Amazon.com*; *www.BN.com*; *www.deepershopping.com*, and wherever books are sold.)

The Other Side of Life – Over 60? God Still Has a Plan for You, by Rev. Warren C. Biebel, Jr. – Drawing on biblical examples and his 60-plus years of pastoral experience, Rev. Biebel helps older (and younger) adults understand God's view of aging and the rich life available to everyone who seeks a deeper relationship with God as they age. Rev. Biebel explains how to: Identify God's ongoing plan for your life; Rely on faith to manage the anxieties of aging;

Form positive, supportive relationships; Cultivate patience; Cope with new technologies; Develop spiritual integrity; Understand the effects of dementia; Develop a Christ-centered perspective of aging. (Printed book: $10.95; PDF eBook: $6.95; both together: $15.00 – direct from publisher; printed books and eBooks available at *www.Amazon.com*; *www.BN.com*; *www.deepershopping.com*, and wherever books are sold.)

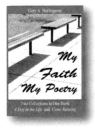

My Faith, My Poetry, by Gary A. Burlingame – This unique book of Christian poetry is actually two in one. The first collection of poems, A Day in the Life, explores a working parent's daily journey of faith. The reader is carried from morning to bedtime, from "In the Details," to "I Forgot to Pray," back to "Home Base," and finally to "Eternal Love Divine." The second collection of poems, Come Running, is wonder, joy, and faith wrapped up in words that encourage and inspire the mind and the heart. (Printed book: $10.95; PDF eBook: $6.95; both together: $13.95 – direct from publisher; printed books and eBooks available at *www.Amazon.com*; *www.BN.com*; *www.deepershopping.com*, and wherever books are sold.)

On Eagles' Wings, by Sara Eggleston – One woman's life journey from idyllic through chaotic to joy, carried all the way by the One who has promised to never leave us nor forsake us. Remarkable, poignant, moving, and inspiring, this autobiographical account will help many who are facing difficulties that seem too great to overcome or even bear at all. It is proof that Isaiah 40:31 is as true today as when it was penned, "But they that wait upon the LORD shall renew their strength; they shall mount up with wings as eagles; they shall run, and not be weary; and they shall walk, and not faint." (Printed book: $14.95; PDF eBook: $8.95; both together: $22.95 – direct from publisher; printed books and eBooks available at *www.Amazon.com*; *www.BN.com*; *www.deepershopping.com*, and wherever books are sold.)

Richer Descriptions, by Gary A. Burlingame – A unique and handy manual, covering all nine human senses in seven chapters, for Christian speakers and writers. Exercises and a speaker's checklist equip speakers to engage their audiences in a richer experience. Writing examples and a writer's guide help writers bring more life to the characters and scenes of their stories. Bible references encourage a deeper appreciation of being created by God

for a sensory existence. (Printed book: $15.95; PDF eBook: $8.95; both together: $22.95 – direct from publisher; printed books and eBooks available at *www.Amazon.com*; *www.BN.com*; *www.deepershopping.com*, and wherever books are sold.)

Treasuring Grace, by Rob Plumley and Tracy Roberts – This novel was inspired by a dream. Liz Swanson's life isn't quite what she'd imagined, but she considers herself lucky. She has a good husband, beautiful children, and fulfillment outside of her home through volunteer work. On some days she doesn't even notice the dull ache in her heart. While she's preparing for their summer kickoff at Lake George, the ache disappears and her sudden happiness is mistaken for anticipation of their weekend. However, as the family heads north, there are clouds on the horizon that have nothing to do with the weather. Only Liz's daughter, who's found some of her mother's hidden journals, has any idea what's wrong. But by the end of the weekend, there will be no escaping the truth or its painful buried secrets.

(Printed: $12.95; PDF eBook: $7.95; both together: $19.95 – direct from publisher; printed books and eBooks available at *www.Amazon.com*; *www.BN.com*; *www.deepershopping.com*, and wherever books are sold.)

From Orphan to Physician – The Winding Path, by Chun-Wai Chan, MD – From the foreword: "In this book, Dr. Chan describes how his family escaped to Hong Kong, how they survived in utter poverty, and how he went from being an orphan to graduating from Harvard Medical School and becoming a cardiologist. The writing is fluent, easy to read and understand. The sequence of events is realistic, emotionally moving, spiritually touching, heartwarming, and thought provoking. The book illustrates . . . how one must have faith in order to walk through life's winding path." (Printed book: $14.95; PDF eBook: $8.95; both together: $22.95 – direct from publisher; printed books and eBooks available at *www.Amazon.com*; *www.BN.com*; *www.deepershopping.com*, and wherever books are sold.)

12 Parables, by Wayne Faust – Timeless Christian stories about doubt, fear, change, grief, and more. Using tight, entertaining prose, professional musician and comedy performer Wayne Faust manages to deal with difficult concepts in a simple, straightforward way. These are stories you can read aloud over and over—to your spouse, your family, or in a group setting. Packed with emotion and just enough mystery to keep you wondering, while

providing lots of points to ponder and discuss when you're through, these stories relate the gospel in the tradition of the greatest speaker of parables the world has ever known, who appears in them often. (Printed book: $14.95; PDF eBook: $8.95; both together: $22.95 – direct from publisher; printed books and eBooks available at *www.Amazon.com*; *www.BN.com*; *www.deepershopping.com*, and wherever books are sold.)

The Answer is Always "Jesus," by Aram Haroutunian, who gave children's sermons for 15 years at a large church in Golden, Colorado—well over 500 in all. This book contains 74 of his most unforgettable presentations—due to the children's responses. Pastors, homeschoolers, parents who often lead family devotions, or other storytellers will find these stories, along with comments about props and how to prepare and present them, an invaluable asset in reconnecting with the simplest, most profound truths of Scripture, and then to envision how best to communicate these so even a child can understand them. (Printed book: $12.95; PDF eBook: $8.95; both together: $19.95 – direct from publisher; printed books and eBooks available at *www.Amazon.com*; *www.BN.com*; *www.deepershopping.com*, and wherever books are sold.)

Handbook of Faith, by Rev. Warren C. Biebel, Jr. – The New York Times World 2011 Almanac claimed that there are 2 billion, 200 thousand Christians in the world, with "Christians" being defined as "followers of Christ." The original 12 followers of Christ changed the world; indeed, they changed the history of the world. So this author, a pastor with over 60 years' experience, poses and answers this logical question: "If there are so many 'Christians' on this planet, why are they so relatively ineffective in serving the One they claim to follow?" Answer: Because, unlike Him, they do not know and trust the Scriptures, implicitly. This little volume will help you do that. (Printed book: $8.95; PDF eBook: $6.95; both together: $13.95 – direct from publisher; printed books and eBooks available at *www.Amazon.com*; *www.BN.com*; *www.deepershopping.com*, and wherever books are sold.)

Pieces of My Heart, by David L. Wood – Eighty-two lessons from normal everyday life. David's hope is that these stories will spark thoughts about God's constant involvement and intervention in our lives and stir a sense of how much He cares about every detail that is important to us. The piece missing represents his son, Daniel, who died in a fire shortly before his first birthday. (Printed book: $16.95; PDF eBook: $8.95; both to-

gether: $24.95 – direct from publisher; printed books and eBooks available at *www.Amazon.com*; *www.BN.com*; *www.deepershopping.com*, and wherever books are sold.)

Unless otherwise noted on the site itself, shipping is free for all products purchased through www.healthylifepress.com.

Dream House, by Justa Carpenter – Written by a New England builder of several hundred homes, the idea for this book came to him one day as he was driving that came to him one day as was driving from one job site to another. He pulled over and recorded it so he would remember it, and now you will remember it, too, if you believe, as he does, that ". . . He who has begun a good work in you will complete it until the day of Jesus Christ." (Printed book: $10.95; PDF eBook: $6.95; both together: $13.95 – direct from publisher; printed books and eBooks available at *www.Amazon.com*; *www.BN.com*; *www.deepershopping.com*, and wherever books are sold.)

A Simply Homemade Clean, by homesteader Lisa Barthuly – "Somewhere along the path, it seems we've lost our gumption, the desire to make things ourselves," says the author. "Gone are the days of 'do it yourself.' Really . . . why bother? There are a slew of retailers just waiting for us with anything and everything we could need; packaged up all pretty, with no thought or effort required. It is the manifestation of 'progress' . . . right?" I don't buy

that!" Instead, Lisa describes how to make safe and effective cleansers for home, laundry, and body right in your own home. This saves money and avoids exposure to harmful chemicals often found in commercially produced cleansers. (**Full-color** printed book: $16.99; PDF eBook: $6.95; both together: $22.95 – direct from publisher; printed books and eBooks available at *www.Amazon.com*; *www.BN.com*; *www.deepershopping.com*, and wherever books are sold.)

The Secret of Singing Springs, by Monte Swan – One Colorado family's treasure-hunting adventure along the trail of Jesse James. The Secret of Singing Springs is written to capture for children and their parents the spirit of the hunt—the hunt for treasure as in God's Truth, which is the objective of walking the Way of Wisdom that is described in Proverbs. (Printed book: $12.95, PDF eBook: $9.99; both together: $19.99 – direct from publisher; printed books and eBooks available at *www.Amazon.com*; *www.BN.com*; *www.deepershopping.com*, and wherever books are sold.)

God Loves You Circle, by Michelle Johnson – Daily inspiration for your deeper walk with Christ. This collection of short stories of Christian living will make you laugh, make you cry, but most of all make you contemplate—the meaning and value of walking with the Master moment-by-moment, day-by-day. (**Full-color** printed book: $17.95; PDF eBook: $9.99; both together: $22.99 – direct from publisher; printed books and eBooks available at *www.Amazon.com*; *www.BN.com*; *www.deepershopping.com*, and wherever books are sold.)

Our God-Given Senses, by Gary A. Burlingame – Did you know humans have NINE senses? The Bible draws on these senses to reveal spiritual truth. We are to taste and see that the Lord is a good. We are to carry the fragrance of Christ. Our faith is produced upon hearing. Jesus asked Thomas to touch him. God created us for a sensory experience and that is what you will find in this book. (Printed book: $12.99; PDF eBook: $9.99; both together: $19.99 – direct

from publisher; printed books and eBooks available at *www.Amazon.com*; *www.BN.com*; *www.deepershopping.com*, and wherever books are sold.)

Vows, a Romantic novel by F. F. Whitestone – When the police cruiser pulled up to the curb outside, Faith Framingham's heart skipped a beat, for she could see that Chuck, who should have been driving, was not in the vehicle. Chuck's partner, Sandy, stepped out slowly. Sandy's pursed lips and ashen face spoke volumes. Faith waited by the front door, her hands clasped tightly, to counter the fact that her mind was already reeling. "Love never fails." A compelling story. (Printed book: $12.99; PDF eBook: $9.99; both together, $19.99 – direct from publisher; printed books and eBooks available at *www.Amazon.com*; *www.BN.com*; *www.deepershopping.com*, and wherever books are sold.)

Unless otherwise noted on the site itself, shipping is free for all products purchased through www.healthylifepress.com.

Worth the Cost?, by Jack Tsai, MD – The author was happily on his way to obtaining the American Dream until he decided to take seriously Jesus' command, "Come, follow me." Join him as he explores the cost of medical education and Christian discipleship. Planning to serve God in your future vocation? Take care that your desires do not get side-tracked by the false promises of this world. What you should be doing now so when you are done with your training you will still want to serve God. (Printed book: $12.99, PDF eBook: $9.99; both together: $19.99 – direct from publisher; printed books and eBooks available at *www.Amazon.com*; *www.BN.com*; *www.deepershopping.com*, and wherever books are sold.)

Nature: God's Second Book – An Essential Link to Restoring Your Personal Health and Wellness: Body, Mind, and Spirit, by Elvy P. Rolle – An inspirational book that looks at nature across the seasons of nature and of life. It uses the biblical Emmaus Journey as an analogy for life's journey, and offers ideas for using nature appreciation and exploration to reduce life's stresses. The

author shares her personal story of how she came to grips with this concept after three trips to the emergency room. (**Full-color** printed book: $12.99; PDF eBook $8.99; both together: $16.99 – direct from publisher; printed books and eBooks available at *www.Amazon.com*; *www.BN.com*; *www.deepershopping.com*, and wherever books are sold.)

He Waited, by LaDonna Cooper – Inspires readers to wait upon the Lord for His best for them; stresses the importance of putting God's purpose above one's own; emphasizes that God's love is unconditional; demonstrates the wisdom of waiting, through a combination of positive insights, encouragement, biblical examples and principles. Decorated with original poetry by the author. For singles and others who are waiting. Distributed primarily through *www.Amazon.com*. (Printed book: $10.99; PDF eBook: $9.99; both together: $15.99 – direct from publisher; printed books and eBooks available at *www.Amazon.com*; *www.BN.com*; *www.deepershopping.com*, and wherever books are sold.)

Seasonal

The Big Black Book – What the Christmas Tree Saw, by Rev. Warren C. Biebel, Jr. – An original Christmas story, from the perspective of the Christmas tree. This little book is especially suitable for parents to read to their children at Christmas time or all year-round. (**Full-color** printed book: $9.95; PDF eBook: $4.95; both together: $12.95 – direct from publisher; printed books and eBooks available at *www.Amazon.com*; *www.BN.com*; *www.deepershopping.com*, and wherever books are sold.)

CPSIA information can be obtained
at www.ICGtesting.com
Printed in the USA
LVOW10s2005090118
562398LV00022B/331/P